Living in Croesor

by the same author

MEMOIRS OF A PUBLIC BABY (*Faber & Faber*)

THE LOWER VIEW (*Faber & Faber*)

STEINER'S TOUR (*Olympia Press, Paris*)

Philip O'Connor

PHILIP O'CONNOR

Living in Croesor

HUTCHINSON OF LONDON

HUTCHINSON & CO. (*Publishers*) LTD
178–202 Great Portland Street, London, W.1

London Melbourne Sydney
Auckland Bombay Toronto
Johannesburg New York

First published 1962

*This book has been set in Bembo type face. It has
been printed in Great Britain by The Anchor Press,
Ltd., in Tiptree, Essex, on Antique Wove paper.*

Respectfully, to the people of Croesor and to Edith Young, who first told me about it; Ruth Elias, who enabled us to come here; Margaret Williams, who makes strangers welcome.

Acknowledgements

To the late Bob Owen, Esq., OBE, for help in the section on himself; Dyfed Evans, Esq., for permission to use Mr. Owen's account of his life as told to Mr. Evans for the paper *Y Cymro*; Mrs. Margaret Williams for translating the same; Showell Styles, Esq., for material used in the section on himself; Clough Williams-Ellis, Esq., CBE, FRIBA, for material used in the section on himself; the people of Croesor for their kind co-operation; and the B.B.C. for allowing me to use transcripts of tape-recordings from 'Croesor'. The photographs are by Owain Tudur Owen, Esq.

Permission to quote from the following works has been obtained:

Headlong Down the Years: Annabel & Clough Williams-Ellis. Liverpool University Press

Tao Te Chung: trans. J. J. L. Duyvendak (Wisdom of the East series). John Murray

Illusion and Reality: Christopher Caudwell. Macmillan & Co.

Further Studies in a Dying Culture: Christopher Caudwell. The Bodley Head Ltd.

Contents

Illustrations

Foreword

There's no doubt but that the pomp of writing as well as much of its 'urgency' comes from the socially equivocal position of the writer. He is to be sincere, but he is also to be professional; the incompatibility of these two demands seems to have struck few writers—in print. In fact I once suggested something of this to an editor (Spender); I mentioned, I think, that payment somewhat inhibited my freedom in writing: I should of course have added that lack of payment would altogether have prevented it. Spender, in a letter which I have lost and can only paraphrase from memory, turned my plaint into an accusation. He didn't at all sympathize. And yet, isn't the difficulty obvious? A writer with a private income is saved the problem, but may suffer from a certain abstraction provided by the financial raft—unless he is extremely intelligent and rather abstract anyway. A writer depending for his survival (and that of his family) upon writing to some extent *pleasingly*, must inch by inch feel himself edging into the ranks of the oldest profession. The tension between the need to be pleasing and the equal need to satisfy himself by being honest inflates his writing into rhetoric and that professional urgency which is the curse of much fiction and the disaster of most personal confessions. The urgency is actually that of the writer's tension between two stools, not that of the importance of the truth he has to tell.

I make the above point because in writing this book I have, more than once, wondered why I should continue to think and to recount details of my 'personal' life for, obviously, money as well as—often—my personal satisfaction. True, I have to do something 'for money', or I couldn't live, and that I chose writing and not fighting, for instance,

13

suggests writing may have chosen me and that that was the most suitable profession. All the same, that does not explain everything. I cannot write fiction; I must admit that life, as written by me, appears sufficiently fictive; is fictive as lived, not only as recounted. To write fiction one must have a sense of the basic reality of life, which I lack; life appears to me to be arbitrary, planless, devoid of intelligence; I am not at all certain where the division between life and fiction lies, if it lies anywhere properly. So the reality of my life and of what I see of the lives of others is as fictive to me—more so, in fact—than most novels. In most novels, in fact, I see a dingy superstition at work in the strident *'arrivisme'* of the numberless states of being so breathlessly advertised, in the constant pressure of apocalyptic moments of truth, in the sad salad of souls always being freshly dressed for no one's consumption. There is a hectic pseudo-verisimilitude that keeps the real thing (of Tolstoy's, for instance) well off the page. So my 'private' life is as 'public' and, in the contemplation, almost as fictive as that of the second Mrs. Tanqueray. It is, therefore, the proper meat for my humble dressing, the proper material for what makes, I suppose, my kind of journalism. But haven't there always been some to whom life does lack this *religion* of reality (as I like to think of it)? Frankly I have no doubts about the value of a total lack of discretion about one's private life; I regard it as therapeutic not only for the writer but for the reader. I regard private life as the ulcer in the social stomach, the source or concentrate of all misery, the reactionary and unhygienic factor, the conspiracy against progress. To be 'tactful' is to subscribe to a very poor, very sordid, conspiracy, to close one's mind to the far spaces and to one's fellow men.

My lack of discretion is not total, because the state of things is as it is; I favour instead a Trojan-horse strategy. Or, in alignment with the progressive revelation of the female body to assembled males in special places of entertainment, I favour progressive self-revelation in my more 'intellectual' branch of the business, obviously less courageous (therefore much more self-consciously desperate) than that of the strip-tease department.

Of course, the self does tend to disappear through constant practice of these operations; that was not the least of the practitioner's intentions. Having decided that the self hurled at him, like a rotten tomato at a disliked actor, had little to do with 'him' (and his esoteric mumbo-jumbo is mainly an attempt to explain this anomaly), he is bent upon reducing it to nothing by artful presentation of it. I like an unknown self, whom I then needn't bother to like; a known self demands stupendous nursing, and much sacrifice. The self is kept unknown by all conceptions of it being given verbal representation.

Good taste, while admirable in a superficially aesthetic manner, is the final obstacle to good sense; hence some justification for the beats, and for some of their especially intelligent writers such as, for instance, Mr. Mailer. So long as his honesty doesn't, through that vertigo of impotence usually honesty's reward, become drugged into rhetoric and the genial desperation of the comfortable demagogue, he will continue to be useful. Mr. Sillitoe is another in this engagement.

Of course, the question of good taste is the question also of the commercially sustained sacrosanctity of the individual, an old cripple whose wounds must be guarded from the eyes of other cripples lest there be general despair. The individual is as commercial an enterprise as a tea company: and, to reappear at the commencement of this argument, his unwrapping on television being now an accredited business, my own unwrapping can surely no longer be attacked—as it was last time I published a book. I must be in the same line of business, I see at last.

So, like every tradesman—as all writers and artists must be—I can only fall back on the old defence of all tradesmen: these goods are authentic, and come straight to you from my garden factory. If religion is business, I mustn't mind being, in my small way, business. However, I do.

My original purpose, apart from elements of exhibitionism, self-pity, and the wish to make some money, in publishing my first book of autobiography was to give vent to certain hatreds that had prevented the smooth course of, I think, certain loves. My hatreds included that of privacy, the English *chef d'œuvre*, and the holy cult of combative individualism, its justification. I wanted then, and for as long as I can remember, a public family. I continue to want it, and I know that it will come, no doubt a long time after my death.

In the general scheme of contemporary writing, including writing for the theatre, there are and have for a long time been two main divisions: the politically progressive, which deals in units one may call conservative or conventional, and the politically unconscious, whose units are progressive. The latter is often styled 'decadent', and its material is, often, the experimentally lived lives of its writers. We must realize that politically progressive people will most usually have conventional private lives and be conventional in everything but their politics; the others, the experimentalists, the 'uncommitted', will be— or may be—politically rather hopeless. This comes, of course, from the traditional dichotomy of thought and action. I mention this because it is related to another 'guilt' I have in writing professionally. My first desire was to do, not to think; to be an active revolutionary, in fact. That I have not become one and am, in fact, among the least inclined of writers to be one now, is not due to any change of opinions. I am more than ever convinced of the need for socialism, and for the nurture of the true individual from the true community, instead of the anarchic tank in the jungle we have today. But revolution, through constitutional or other means, is now a profession calling for a special kind of person, an expert. I have been forced to discover many years ago that I am not one of them. With a mind like a haystack in a gale, only now and then manageable under a rapidly applied canvas covering, with almost no sense of direction, with regular stupefaction before the facts of individual strategy, with astonishment that *increases* at the spectacle of human ploys, I would be like a blind elephant in a regiment of sharpshooters were I to attempt revolutionary activity. Writing seems a poor second-best beside this, possibly, romantic fiction—as it must be to others. I have only one comfort and one 'justification': I know what I do, but never how I do it (or fail). My star, my target attracting me, is some perception of a non-competitive society: the errors in this conception will be numberless, and a truth may slenderly emerge—there is no guarantee. I find it astonishing that so little is done towards the realization, intellectually, of this human destiny. When one considers the new world of socialism, with its limitless possibilities in peace and creation, and then considers, for instance, the Labour Party, with its windy rhetoric and intellectual cupboard life, one is obviously considering two nearly unrelated things; one forgets, in looking at the Labour Party, that one may be looking at a very able servant; not one's own, though.

When I lived in London I found that I was engaged in an unrewarding sustenance of a 'revolutionary' personality; I was busily failing at that thin imitation of the real thing, busily treading water and confusing self-conception with work—self-conception is hard work of a kind, of course. I then accepted *escapism*, long ago encouraged, of course, by being told it was impossible. I decided to go thoroughly stupid in fact, to let the concepts melt in the heat of the sun, to let the ideas, mangy and on heat as they so easily can be in an urban civilization that refuses to advance, wander abroad and possibly perish. To be as stupid as one is seems to me an essential achievement, and a very delightful one; it brings peace. I have, all my life, been forced to move into apparently unpropitious circumstances offering, again apparently, no support to my 'personality'; for my personality quickly congeals into an unmanageable stock that must, at all costs, be unwrapped, undone, unwound and redistributed to the fields. I find it essential periodically not to know anything at all; this, of course, is the substitute and intellectualized function of the sexual orgasm and, in older age, I find that the orgasm increasingly takes over its proper function. But when I was young I was a marvellously fierce puritan, and then developed this habit of total change every few years. The need to wrench out of all that I think I know, out of all familiar people and places—it is as necessary as breathing. In my personal life, for instance, I find any constant expression alarmingly imprisoning; I include the expression of emotions.

Therefore I came to Croesor, and found a place in which my barnacled personality could once again find its fruitful grave. I found here a people of relative simplicity, of fresh and uncontrived personality, with a lyrical attitude to life. I almost certainly have oversimplified them, have, perhaps, idealized them; but I think overestimation of people is far more realistic than that sick, banal and still fatuously fashionable 'disillusionment' anent them. We are, to this day, each other's undiscovered countries; discovery alone is enough to make the territory fair, and it had better be: because we are, in these competitive days, *alarmingly* alike.

If this book has a theme at all, it is the theme of the superiority of commonness over that species of 'individuality' whose spurious values still blind people to one another. *Only* in the recognition of blessed human commonness, which perception liberates all energies, can fruitful and pacific uncommonness be nurtured. One is *anyone*; it is the allegedly egotistical study of oneself (which is of one's self-conception) that tells one so; until oneself and other people have, really, very little out of common. And this had better be the case, lest something come down from the skies.

PHILIP O'CONNOR

PART ONE

Croesor

I

London

EXPRESSION and depression (life and death!) compose the basic burden of our lives; some would substitute 'impression' for 'depression'. But their impending coalescence at this long end of an epoch makes of 'impression' an all too hopeful version of the truth. Impression is aborted in impressionism which, I believe, is patently remote from expression, a mere throwing back of the ball: the shadows behind that game are undigested science and hostile reality. To articulate is festive; in the enormous boom of human chatter, printed or spoken, expression is becoming almost impossibly clinical. But for the stranded outsider (who is properly the insider *manqué*), that parody of a human being with too much honour called an observer, there is no other path to follow. We flatter ourselves that we are entered into a period in the arts of free expression. This is but a fashionable gloss upon our pretensions to freedom in general. As free speech writhes fetchingly around unfree action, so liberated art hides the absence of living meaning. Tolstoy thought the answer lay in a deliberately moral art; but there we would have but the continuation of the parallelism of life and morality for the reader only too easily to be able to evade the morality, as the experienced fellow does in life. We have to return to the well-known truism—that the value of life, whose virtue it is a technological matter to apply to society, must by the artist be perceived and creatively rendered. Having lost beauty, however, we have lost sight of that virtue. Once we had the divine; divinity thrilled art, and art displayed man to divinity. The divine is gone, half-way down the skies to humanity, which has not yet caught it in social arms. Hence the opera of artistic integrity in lieu of wider justifications; which is also the pantomime of artistic insignificance.

In London, where the historical bones are nourished on the contemporary flesh, expression is especially devalued. It has become a personal manifestation of immunity to impression, if often in the guise of sympathetic sensitivity. The rattle of its shot ricocheting from the hard walls (smiling) of one personality to the other makes that uproar we are beginning to confuse with 'life'. The terror is thought- and perception-breeding silence, and the identifiable horror of sub-identity. The substitute for community is the noise necessitated by its absence. Vitality, sometimes a superstition of the dead, is everywhere emulated; one may there hear skeletons rattling in dustbins, in the truly awful silence of this social din. So a new seat of reflexes is established, on the outer periphery of the cerebral consciousness, where traffic is immediate and allusive only in its effects: the cutaneous timpani of the lively corpses. Along comes the hangover where nerves writhe with exhaustion and brilliance falls like a dinner-plate. Then we hear the tom-toms of revengeful humanity through the night and much of the Lawrentian diagnosis validated. The unexpressed thought stalks through the mind in horrifying garments from the wardrobe of repression—as for exploitation of 'profoundly contemporary art'. The human quality of expression is distended to its inhuman quantity; we meet to enhance the value of our separateness, the most grotesque medal of honour we have ever awarded ourselves, which a cat would disdain: excelsior to death, a really *sterling* community.

I've spent about twenty of forty-four years in London, and cannot remember one of them that had the important quality of naturalness. The twenty years were in several stages. I first met it as a drawing-room in a Cromwell Road flat, and I'm sure the lack of air was in part accountable for my sensation (rather than sense) of the brilliance of the apartment. Lights glowed on soft carpets, whose emanation from my mother is now evident enough. A Paris drawing-room, for instance, of a few months later was quite different; brilliant without being soft, as though a razor had trimmed the chiaroscuro away, making for the separation of colours and the vivacity of forms, and a

tonic refrigeration of French voices. Then at seven I descended into
London as a basement in Dean Street, having been arrested by England
in the quietly ominous sliding and whispering of the Folkestone boat-
train. I served I think a year's sentence in the cellar; the milk-can
clatter on the pavements was insulated with dampness in the air,
and colours committed incest to avoid identification or marriage.

At around eleven and twelve I descended into London from the
Surrey hills occasionally to meet my guardian; London then more
explicitly conveyed to me its terrible combination of enervation and
cerebral excitation. First my 'personality' was by the brushings of
people and traffic inflamed to exalted significance; then I became hot-
faced, my country life became an impediment of speech and behaviour,
and I quickly dwindled to the feeling of being a small pebble on a
shore made desolate precisely by the quantity of other pebbles . . .
smoothed to 'decent' anonymity. This process, thirty-odd years later,
is become modified but is essentially the same. London is still an
indoors enormous; as in a car 30 m.p.h. feels fast there, so gestures,
expressions and thoughts which at home—in the country—can suffer
the gestations proper for their maturation, in London speed to a
frenzy: though their actual development is, if anything, slower by
reason of their deracination; roots, like intestines, are portable in
London and sockets to plug into for communication are wonderfully
hidden.

At seventeen I entered the private shrubbery of my mother's little
encampment, for her to die therein; London wore the face of The
Waste Land, and I reeled out of it on the tramping road. Off to France,
in 1937, I returned to the hotter nightmare of the early war years
where communication wore the simpering ineffability of conscientious classlessness. It was useful to have men equal for the duration, but
it made them curiously shy, and a sigh of relief went up when the
bowlers and caps came out again, and shopkeepers could be forthright
(i.e. rude), conveying self-respect. Around thirty I did my stint in the
depths, spiritually warm and physically impossible; the slime sticking
to me, I made the semi-heights of Hampstead, where culture is demi-
haute couture. There we continued to wave the branches of understanding at each other, to preclude shattering expression. I spent

hours in the bath-tub, but discovered hygiene to be no substitute for humanity, which was reduced to an auspicious and continuous leaking through the armour of rectitude. Righteously, men clang in their contretemps like the armoured knights of old. London reached the nadir of its dehydrated phenomenalism—only the slums maintain a species of sap.

This, the penultimate bout of my suffering the great city, made clearer to me the quality of its (middle-class) expression that I had always found so frustrating. As in the encased silence of the Folkestone boat-train, against which the whiskers of mutual speech could be heard ruminatively rubbing, so the proper and decent London middle-class man impinges upon statements to withdraw from exciting meaning. My comparison was still, I think, with France (North). I reached the conclusion of a satisfactory explanation of this indirectness (and 'impassioned'—i.e. congested—pseudo-directness) in terms of the relationship of the Londoner to his environment, compared with that of the Frenchman to his. The Londoner is half of it, half nebulously—religiously, one may say—against it. Environment and he are a pair of Siamese twins, living in strangely physical sin. He has no outline, instead walks in the nimbus of the implicit, daring no more than the semi-explicit; realism subsumes into the agreeable hum of his voice and over-deliberate continuity of his thought (to evade the penalty of suffering the sensible impact of one thought to another, and of one person on another). In a word, English individualism (and individualism is created out of community and environment) was adhesive to English environment, because it lacked its creative traffic with it. Whereas the French, blithe if rather thin in nervous covering, might still tock with stalactitic definitiveness upon the cobbles, speak and close car-doors with an elegant and succinct spring, like the verse of Manley Hopkins. The French still appear to *deal* with their environment, to the mutual refreshment of each; whereas the English grudgingly adhere to and agitate against it. So muted is the essence of English lives, where competition, through an ancient versatility and a reckless virtuosity, has become now confined in too many overcoats of restrictions for it to move.

I'm certain it was this mutedness, to which I was congenitally allergic, that contrived most of my inversion. As a boy I noted how my spontaneous actions were deemed mad, whereas my wicked diplomacy (which exhausted me) was deemed sensible and even charming. Hence I acquired restraint, which agreed with me less than with my fellows more nationally gifted. Restraint, from the fury encased, bred such insulating intellectualism as I now suffer from. What appalled me in my sorrows was the epicene brand of ritualistic and ineffectual rebelliousness considered the thing by a cosy Establishment, still unchanged.

London was like the inside of a smooth chromium tube. The streets were *vastly* impersonal (unless you caught sight of old commercial ghosts leering in the cornices), and the architecture heterogeneous—pockets of dead souls in acres of the vulgar and imported present. Solitude was first densely silent, then surrealistically garrulous. Social manners, soft clothes on hard bones, were the ultimate in exploiting the means of communication for the essence of separation. As a child such rigid poise—even in fluency—terrified me; as though I'd gone out walking and met perambulating cathedrals looking at me with coloured glass eyes, with dim rumours of esoteric services deep within. But when I entered one after another such a cathedral, I found but a rusty machine, forlorn as a kittenless cat, within: the machine to issue to the world notices of subliminal existence, and perhaps to advertise a party on a death-bed. Which may lead us to reflect that when people lose the power of quick and whole reaction, 'they', the real people, become covered with a thick psychological architecture, which art is forced to waste its time in dramatizing *en bloc*, or scraping away to reach an infinitely rare, infinitely abstract, essence. To such an extent is this development upon us that the covering ('psychological') has come to mean the truth, and the truth has become the myth. But the youngest generation of writers appears to be in the process of being able to forget so many imponderable subtleties in order to grasp and make real again some rough shape of the original.

I have suggested the over-covering of a past competitive virtuosity as a cause (or description in depth) of the Londoner's muted communication services (across which, like poppies in a cornfield, the oddly graceful, oddly aesthetic, true Cockney speech may remind us of something better). That is the point: a maturedly commercial people is, in tired time, atomized into incommunicative parts. Paris is sharp but adolescent in the manner of luxe with which it displays its wares, in the *brio* and romanticism with which it sings its finance; London maturedly houses its commercial and financial life as a ship houses its engines. Only a tremor indicates their deep presence; the passengers smile on deck in a manner feyly unrelated to the motive power that sends them along. To see the engines one must crash through many decks of economic layers, and leave temporarily at least the world of passengers. I dislike London because it is paramountly a centre of buying and selling; and this fact springs directly to mind as the cause of the general incommunication. I learned that one had to sell to live; I still think that selling is a very disgusting operation; that we all do it means that we are all, to an extent, disgusting. Obviously a fairly firm picture of a world in which one didn't sell and buy has reached us from both the future and the past, from which we can make a standard. Heaven, also, has for long been such a place from which even the most delicately equivocal transaction of marriage is barred. Selling is, of course, an operation distinct from making; only the chronological sequence provides the darkening association. Artists know, or should know, what a nuisance it is when art has no integrated place in the community. Demand and supply are industriously co-opted for identification with buying and selling by apologists of the system; their identification is sophistical.

Selling is, to repeat, a disgusting operation to any normal person; the suppression of this awareness must account for the proliferation of 'poetical' philosophies and rotundly rhetorical ethics that 'justify' or explain it, since the Founder of the faith to which their several authors so agilely subscribe omitted to do so. If this allergy to trade be deemed snobbish, I would then be reminded of a few of the valid elements in snobbery; which is, however, the worst word for the matter. Selling involves duplicity in the euphemistically styled 'description' of one's wares; it involves to a catastrophic extent the inclusion of oneself in them, especially in the arts (at the personality level; in employment, physically and mentally). It involves a grotesque distortion of one's true feelings about 'useful' people; it opens the door to every degree of equivocation, and it provides the compulsive transgressor with the succubus of his mortal life, the soul: a metaphorical growth contrived from imaginings of one's unemployed integrity.

In the thirties, when the market wasn't as good as it is now, this attitude was not considered as eccentric as it is today. So many were unsaleable that a virtue for this condition was more or less necessary to find. Today the lifting of a well-known eyebrow has market value; hence the ethics of selling are brilliantly ignored. Hence it was with an aplomb based not entirely on the allergy mentioned that I was an angry young man rather before this commodity was fetching good prices. I had support in the times. I have failed since to see reason, however (not being quite cross-eyed), and am become relatively incomprehensible in my *pudeurs*. So be it. A love of money's uses doesn't help, especially when it stops short of persuading me to the general artful emulation of a nice chop for the public. A further inconvenient exile was from my immediate precursors' worship of integrity (their own), tail end of the art-for-art's sakers; the ineffability of a proposed true self left me cold, because the self is not properly to be separated from every sly thing it's up to—hence, as above, the necessary metaphorization of it as soul. The cradle and the jungle of all these goings-on was grey London, a stone-and-concrete mess, wherein the alive, the lyrical, has its ghosts as the paper bags blown skilfully along the cold streets by, one may conceive, mocking and exiled humanity.

Inevitably I pictured ideal places of an opposite character. Nostalgically, it was France; but a later visit modified the memory, though I still love that country. Then it became Suffolk, where I lived for two or three years, until I noted the encroachment of London on a people not alien to the enemy. Rumours of North Wales had reached me in 1954, but in a bout of tramping that year I pusillanimously opted for the home comforts I had left.

But in 1958 I was fortunate enough (at the age of forty-two) to become attached to a girl of nineteen who entirely satisfied my curious demands of innocence without stupidity or British faery; I mean positive innocence, being clarity. This happy reminder that I was not dead, after my sojourn in places of rectitude, inflamed me to the desire and pursuit of the whole. She didn't reject me, and I still occasionally concentrate on finding excuses for her interest, when they appear to me to be necessary; but this is more than 'occasionally'. Perhaps that she was practically an orphan helped her acceptance; orphans, actual or circumstantial, are more courageous in their responses, lacking the torpor induced by the conspiratorial security offered, today, by parentage. They are remarkably contemporary people also, compared with the conventionally parented. Perhaps I should enlarge a little on this romance, since it is quite relevant to our later residence in Croesor; in doing so I shall be, of course, offending with my so-personal confidences such critics suffering from their inhibitory over-valuation as the one who said he had surely never heard of a decent writer who had done the same; forgetting, thereby, every writer of any value at all. For whether we appear in the clothes of our characters, in our personal style of writing, or through our direct confessions, we appear. The impersonal writer is the pseudo-objective hack.

I first met N——, then (who is half French, and to whom I restored her French name), when I was an eccentric cottager in Suffolk and she a schoolgirl of eleven in the adjacent village. She made an impression on me because she appeared neither astonished nor amused at an appearance I was only too willing to exploit as a clown's armour against the usual depredations of 'understanding'; furthermore, she didn't even descend to the latter. She merely saw; today one of our rarest feats. I met her again seven years later when she was returned from France to Suffolk, in the home of her step-father, and I was collecting material on a motorized bicycle for my *Lower View*; then she did laugh, because I was unintentionally funny on the dangerous vehicle. I was very high, as though on a camel, and the creature had the habit of sudden acceleration that made my verticality precarious. I met her finally when I was staying with my friends the Lowsons and, after some opposition, got what I wanted. Uniquely in my life, 'it' hasn't changed in its desirability and value because, whatever it may be (I think the lingua franca of exiles and the resulting dislike of social diplomacy), we have it in common. She hitched me, re-connected me to whatever I am; and really there is nothing of what's available better to be. Re-connection to it was, for me, the end of a long and involved pilgrimage in a maze; it meant at last coming home, and thereby going ahead. The prescription needs no recommending, especially today when young people are so much more sensible than their elders in being guided by the linked heart and sexual desire to the woman or man they can love. I'm sure that never have so few 'good' matches been made as today; this, the moral disaster in the eyes of the ancient camels of propriety that still obstruct our ways, is truly the triumph of sense and the opener of the eye to beauty again. Hence, I'm fairly happy.

Meeting N—— meant the reopening of diplomatic relations (at least) with 'the world', whence I'd withdrawn my emissaries for some time. But I could do this only from a place I could call my own, which could never be in London, or even in Suffolk, where the old parcel of me had been laid too long. So though we at first set up house in Lambs Conduit Street, which is a conduit where no lambs would care to go, we itched to get away into fresh air cleaned, for me, of past associations. There, in spite of an unknown degree of easy contact with my wife, I felt islanded. I felt overwhelmed by the gross untidiness of London's life and appearance; by the drugged propriety of its weeks and the hysterically compensating liberation of its bouts of holiday gregariousness; and with the *literati* I'd never managed at all. Roundly generalizing (an adventure lacking in these days of mousy particularization), I considered them to be brilliantly euphemistic about their function, poised between commodity and 'integrity' status, discreetly valuable about purposes which mightn't bare the light of my consciousness. With their few remaining existentialist teeth they were still gripping the old cultural raft floating gently out to a sea whose change and scope we cannot yet adequately visualize. I exclude such honourable and fine writers as Alan Sillitoe, for instance, and others of the more properly cultural school with whom I was not acquainted. I knew only a handful who were too perilously like a half of myself to allow me to swallow some useful disparagement. It is, I know, tendentious and relative, and perhaps not entirely valid; *sauve qui peut*.

The apathy of these 'prosperous' times has often been commented upon, and the awareness produced cerebrations of 'life' in reaction. The triumphant moral to be deduced from this apathy is that we live neither by bread nor by spirit alone; that where plentiful bread is got without zestful work it does not nourish; that where spirit is got in plenty without bread it does not sustain; that when bread and spirit are properly one we shall live in the new world of a co-operative economy. Till then we're burglars of happiness and journeymen of existence. Those who most cherish some ideal of living (made up largely of childhood memory) in their increasing allergy to misnomered 'reality' (by which we puritanically mean the worst) will try to escape in one of two ways. They may become *overtly* committed to a progressive movement, leading a necessarily social life. Or they may remain 'committed' (the quotes are precautionary) to their ideal, and retire to some lovely and solitary place in order to perfect not necessarily an esoteric conception of 'truth', but possible social implications of that ideal. In other words, they may be field workers or laboratory technicians. The latter group will be highly suspect to the former, and ignored as dreamers by the guardians of the present state; this would be unwise of the guardians but useful to the retreaters. It was Caudwell who propounded the 'paradox' of a man finding his closest communion with his fellows by withdrawing from them—because of the blunting effected by daily communion. Those silly people who vociferously contemn escape in the next breath tell us it is impossible of achievement; good: the impossible is the longest road back, and the most instructive. In effect, those to whom the way of apparent escape comes naturally find a more total escape in so-called committedness, wherein they escape from their talents in being hauled along by their principles: it is given to very few to find talent and principle integrated. The noise of culture is the parody of it. I do believe that Marx advised that artists should be left alone because they were peculiar people. So they are; conformity enforced upon them is even more deleterious to their powers than to those of the more pragmatically operating non-artists. This truth, however, is over-used for the current inflation of artistic personalia. But we must never forget that pulling flowers or people is not the way to make them grow.

Like all the lost, I had cerebrated in manic oases to the near-exhaustion of my powers of survival, which makes for a pathological impatience, when the clock lays out the soul. English tempo had always exacerbated me, first into a neurasthenic virtuosity of response, then into nihilism. Having lived a little too much by what's called the spirit, the body's dominion was forced upon my notice; one makes a tyrant of either by being the protagonist of one. This opened to me the opportunity, which is a godsend to those irreligious still routined in the emotions of religion, of conceiving (never of experiencing) the possible pleasant identity of both. I longed for clear senses, which, in spite of the spectacular achievements of so-called decadents, I believe conducive to the kind of thinking whose good health need not necessarily be equated with conformism; it being a probable sad fact that reactionaries are in a better mental-physical alignment than progressives, who have always been tempted to burn bodily fuel for spiritual fire. Conceptions, in a word, appear to be in an inverse ratio of worth to the constitutions providing them. Or so in the past; the progressive mass now being greater, maybe such fires are employed only for very esoteric advances. I think it will soon be possible to be healthy and progressive—A. S. Neill has practised this assumption for many years. Yet asceticism (broadly speaking, we must include all inverts and 'perverts' among ascetics) is still, isolatedly, the last-ditch technique of 'psychists'—i.e. those who practise the 'conquest' (ignoring) of environment, as opposed to those who recognize in order to change environment.

Wilhelm Reich assessed the percentage of neurotics in the German population, when he was practising in Germany, at over 70 per cent (or possibly higher). By neurotics he meant those whose mental-physical continuity of dynamic reciprocity was disrupted, in terms of the muscular rigidity that provided him with his diagnosis of neurosis. Thinking in terms of mass-neurosis, he inclined to regard individual neurosis, in the more conventional sense, as the failed protest of health. This may be so; nevertheless, if we consider the individual's life tactics in a more pragmatic way we cannot help thinking that so-called 'ordinary people' (as distinct from intellectuals, etc.) have 'managed' a better equilibrium in the resolution of the false dichotomy of body and soul, or body and mind—the spiritual and the physical. What they have lost by so managing is another matter. They have maintained at least an apparent negotiating ability with environment that the more spectacular individual neurotic has not. So, when a man wishes to regain health, as in the thirties, he returns to 'the people', and, if he persist beyond the emoluments of spiritual afflatus and spiritual self-esteem, may be rewarded by finding himself one of them—a point at which the thirties group in the main stopped short. But what 'people'? It was against the background of London and the English that I had cried the wolf of neurosis and acquired the symptoms. I would prefer, perhaps need, a strange people among whom to recuperate. And, remembering the baptismal strategies of the intellectuals of the thirties in the turgid Ganges of the people, I would very positively practise no such tactics, but hope for at most a working and living toleration of myself by them. For 'the people' (as virgins of history?) suspect all suitors, which accounts for the strange charms of politicians.

A bad mind will be an enclosed arena, sealed off for the pedagogical sport, in which a mechanical opposition of abstraction and the concrete will produce the anti-material abstract and the anti-abstract material —i.e. Victorian dead matter and live soul; the effects of atomic physics on this 'thought' haven't yet been noticeable. I suffer very much from this sterile dichotomization of reality. Before a new prospect I composed a spiritual lyric and a material wasteland; their synthesis was Croesor.

Ruth Elias had rented a cottage belonging to the Chapel, and offered it to us; and my friend Edith had been there for several years, for the holidays. Antennae were then at once withdrawn from the London scene; liberated, the city bowled along chirruping, I thought; and I could construe the burden to it (but, oh, I do mean the city as I saw it—should pedants fidget) that my unwilling concern must have been. The people by already being more remote became clearly defined. The buildings were like the teeth of a rake, half snarling, but much more appealing to the skies; some of the silken, light, lyrical humour, the sweet gloss above the smooth roads, like ribbons shone. With me and my concern it lacked shape, was an ominous atmos-phere; without me it was gayer, more careless, more spontaneous and lively. But the people were diminished when I withdrew my fearful *rapport*; neater in their blither passage: how much then of their ailments had been the result of my bondage there? I'd define neither way, for one must be willing to sustain many appearances without forcing any of them off the premises. The people then showed a haunted courage, and the conveyor-belts of their lives rose above the deceptive volition with which my perhaps envious distaste had credited them. I had never acquired their language of *gesture*, a lingua franca among them; I include the gestures in their intonations, the skidding speed of their phrases above the slow, sometimes non-existent, participation of their thought: they were very balletic, and would dislike composers on their stage. The poorer working classes gaze up as from a bowl to the sky; in degree of elevation out of this bowl, the felicities of gesture increased. It was the aim of all to be above the ground; *that* it was that excited a spectral vivacity and an almost posthumous fluency; the choreography had the dancers in thrall, and a pin of a soul nakedly shone through.

But no winds of temporal space blow through the congestion; its self-containedness, the assumption of its inhabitants of being humanly representative *per se*, strikes one as absurd, and even tragic; an island within an island. Hence a source of humour for Londoners is the pretensions to universality of a small community—e.g. *Clochemerle*, the old Pagnol films, any isolated village—that being the mirror image disguised in the reassuring smallness of the amusing community. Urban amusement at villagers is caused by the same inhibited shock of village mentality in themselves; the sophisticated traveller sees little difference, and nothing to laugh at in one that isn't as laughable in the other. True provincialism consists, in city as in village, in the achievement of (to the traveller) a claustrophobic convention of universal normality of the inhabitants. Normality can never be relative. In the arts this 'provincial universalism' is a very diminishing quality, increasingly prevalent in London; Paris had it more spectacularly before the war, and the whole Western world is acquiring it now. What are some of its signs in London behaviour? A mystical avoidance of perspective, of sacrificed spaces and universes, by concentration on detail and particularity—a belief in a Kantian essence to avoid those borders of all phenomena which, so precisely, place phenomena in their proper immensity—in art, the exactitude that *creates* the true vastness of space. (The 'cold war', to the uninitiated not drowned in the historically auspicious' bricks of the situation, pervades the same

C

parochialism.) From this absence of perspective comes the technique occasioned by its loss: a nervous acceleration to avoid considering the direction, which then becomes suitably mystical and Aweful, providing fatalistic chaos-fans with their rabbits' feed. The acceleration produces the polish of sophisticated superficiality; perhaps cars are models for humanity. This gloss finish to the features of busy man has fitted seams for fate-staring crinkles, and can be impressive—it is an American invention, and may be called flexible paralysis. The acceleration subsumes events into moods, rubs the envelope personality (deliriously addressed to whatever gods may be) against its fellows, for further smudging of destinations and inflammation of an hysterically extended moment: isolation of moments from time becomes the mystique of *avant-garde* art. Substituting 'fate's' for 'her', a doggerel composed during one of my domestic incarcerations seems apt:

> 'Locked within her iron embrace
> Doodles of my life I trace.'

I think the practice of autobiography is one of the outcomes of this auspicious stilledness. Comes the slogan of the times: life is *personal*; happily it is more than that, in order, *en route*, to be that. Through persons runs everything; when they block the flowing of history's rivers, they are truly dammed in the moment. Isolated personalism dams history; community engages the flow, for life's hydro-electric force. We have no community, but an *opéra bouffe* of the missing reality. London is the great example of this fact, London being the great conglomeration of disparate solitudes; the Londoner, the busy, vivacious, intelligent metropolitan, becomes the macabrely volatile monument to a great past. But villagers may breathe a contemporary air, though their ideas will be far behind the urban; having missed progress, they may avoid essential anachronism, which always takes the most fashionably modern forms. For the advanced, the contemporary metropolitan man is now also like a taxi-cab, in which he drives a passenger whom he dare not look at, and who haunts him in the night—'himself'. Three elements: the career, situational vehicle; the public persona; the huddled 'soul'. I have exploited poverty to maintain a working coalescence of the three straining parts. Success, which would undo me, is made by my manner of writing implausible. Let us admit, however, that it is precisely *by* doing everything that, in present circumstances, can be done to emulate a community, that Londoners have thereby exemplified their failure. So what there is of community in London (I think almost exclusively among the working classes and, there, in the old-fashioned section) they have created a very lovely myth, in which the word, by so sadly failing to have become flesh, has an iridescent beauty, a Shelleyan delicacy that cannot be forgotten. That can explain why London can also be lovable. There's something of this (tailored) in early T. S. Eliot, before he turned human tragedy into Establishment triumphal arches . . . for the passing through of the soul.

2

First Impressions

WE PACKED *pianissimo*, scooping our possessions out of the present into winged cases, and we left Paddington (a destination-sucked tunnel of glamour) *crescendo*: landed *vibrato* on to the still platform of Penrhyndeudraeth.

The country changes some way past Shrewsbury, and the compartment entering the changed scenery became a stifling box of what we had generally left behind us; we alighted on the platform with a dirty coat of it around us, which took Croesor some weeks altogether to remove. The process was not abrasive but dissolving. But the scenery —the change is from plump complacency (rich apartments holding English beauty, which is delicate, nostalgic, much of it fighting a losing battle against urbanization) to, at first, a high-pitched threnody of 'lostness'. That is but the first impression, relative to the England left. It is the superficial sadness imposed by a less-luxuriant landscape. When the comparison is forgotten, the Welsh scenery enters into its own specific character. To the foreigner, which I must always remain, it becomes 'out of this world': finely strange, spiritous, volatile, in running and eruptive lines, gossamer-fine; it impinges, but in ever increasingly exquisite definitiveness—there's nothing impressionistic about it; I imagine a sort of northern Persia (judging by the Persian painting I have seen). It is the combination of rareness (not faintness) with the very fine linear adventure that makes it so utterly un-English, and that also distinguishes it from Ireland. It is, *vis-à-vis* English landscape, an abstraction; which is important, because the Welsh have an analogous quality. But it is abstract in the proper sense (of a refinement of material), and not in the false, anti-material sense:

36

it would not do to dream it away into transcendentalism, which is so easy to do in Ireland and (with a gasp and determination) in England. The result and corroboration of this is the different tempo, the aerial flexibility of the Welsh character—flexible without being negatively adaptable (being the finest opposite of that). To repeat, to dream this landscape away into faery is to waste it; its character is in its superfine actuality. The air is a colder kind of Grecian air, by cold made purer, without the silver gauze of Greece, but with faint, percussive powders of silver exhausted up, one thinks, from the mountains to the sky, as the winds and moods clearly change. (By 'powder' I mean in contrast to the uniformity of 'gauze'.) It is also clear like the air in certain Italian Primitive paintings, to define the lyricism of, for instance, tree-forms so subtle as to obtrude no boundary of definition from chaos, being organic order. So are Welsh trees or shrubs on the mountainsides.

Mr. Roberts arrived with his taxi to take us to Croesor, a benevolent old gentleman with an expression like that of a winking rose. He threw one or two lines into the pool of our identities, purposes and origins and, in compulsive tribute to the Welsh skill in unobtrusive enquiry, we found ourselves bursting (*anglice*) into information, so that we had the impression of his delicately dusting off the superfluity from his mind. We felt, in a word, our English fatness at once, showing that it was ours mainly by acquisition. That's another refined talent of the Welsh: they remind you of your psychic avoirdupois; none so delicately does this.

After Penrhyndeudraeth we soon left the main road to Caernarvon to go under an arch, suggesting the entrance to a private estate; Mr. Clough Williams-Ellis is not loath to create this impression; the arch is his. Later we did discern an obscure sign (later still hanging pendant from the wall) (later still lost for a while) informing the degradingly curious that the road was a public one to Croesor. We have never felt it to be public road but, being now the other side of the arch, are happy about this.

We passed an apparently elaborate pile on our left, beyond the village of Llanfrothen, called Plâs Brondanw, where Mr. Williams-Ellis of the arch lives in his architectural statement (explaining much of the arch), on to a very narrow road where two cars can pass only

at repeated widenings of the road. We passed a small cottage on the
right that we later called the 'Half-way House', swooped down into a
tree-girded declivity to the left over a bridge where we saw briefly
our first mountain stream (like icy tears running over the slate bed),
steeply uphill, and, by an unexpectedly sharp turn to the left by the
new farmhouse of Mr. Emrys Williams, beheld Croesor's 'High
Street' which, mercifully, is a dead-end on to the 'Roman Road' to
Bedgellert, a track for pedestrians. Facing us, like a ruined stone aunt
knitting in public her dry memories, stood—or pressed—the enormous
chapel, which at first looked to us immensely ugly (which I suppose
it 'is'; such an 'is', however, is safest in quotation marks). We turned
a few yards abruptly up a track to the right and, through the gate
between highish walls, beheld the *triste* dependency of the chapel where
once the ministers had been condemned to live—Ty Capel, like the
chapel, is painted in surely one of the world's worst colour schemes of
brown wood on grey stone. As Mr. Williams-Ellis has lamented, the
Welsh are not ocularly very alive to beauty, or so at least their routine
building would suggest. But I think I culled a nuance of their
character, gradually, out of this placing of bleakly ugly buildings in
opposite landscape: its Puritan core is not remote from the fineness I
have mentioned as belonging to the landscape. The mass around the
core is, of course, due to other factors—chiefly, that most buildings in
Welsh villages date from the sudden incursion of the Industrial
Revolution into Wales. They cannot be said to express indigenous
taste, as do the older Welsh farmhouses and cottages. However, they
must have gone far to spoil it. But Puritanism and the landscape are not
quite correctly, if on the face of it reasonably, to be opposed. For just
a *touch* of the significance of the landscape would be lost by a more
'tasteful' architecture, and would only be found again and aug-
mented by the very best; the very best initially co-operates by
employing local materials, a foundation permitting of an organic
development.

The taxi having departed (and Mr. Roberts having introduced us
to the Welsh manner of receiving payment: absent-mindedly, with
calculation working expertly below the flowing veils of a dreaming
mind), we marched up the long path to the front door (a really fine

one for a cowshed or garden outhouse, in livid brown), and opened it on to desolation, but in a thin layer.

The floors in Ty Capel (like most of those in the village houses) are of dark-grey slate slabs; hence the genius of much interior decoration adds brown woodwork. The effect is indeed depressing, like that of an undertaking business situated at the bottom of a coal-shaft. The left wall on entering Ty Capel (a wall in common with the chapel) was semi-distempered over wallpaper, all rather damp (our friend had been away for six months). The first door to the right gave entry to the 'parlour', a box-like apartment with a metal bedstead in one corner and nothing else. The floor was wooden, all the wood elsewhere brown. The next door led to the kitchen which, the house being jammed against the rock with but a small excavation to allow the light through the window, was extremely dark—we had to have a light on all day. Facing the door was an immense black slate mantelpiece, round an iron range. The furniture consisted of an ailing 'chest', a kitchen table, a promising stuffed Victorian easy chair, a small wooden one and a cherry-pink other. Opening drawers and cupboards, we encountered the final depressant—no, the penultimate—in little tins and jars of damp sugar and rusting salt. The final dolour was offered in the discovery of pencil drawings, a few nudes in that ultimate conception of sadness which makes limbs in the manner of inanimate furniture. These rigid little drawings later reminded me of Reich's theory . . . which I won't interpose here!

I had, as it happened, stayed a night in Ty Capel with Denis Lowson in my tour for *Lower View* of what one critic of that book archly called 'genuine notables' (e.g. such as Bertrand Russell). (He wished to distinguish me from their kind.) Denis psychically collapsed from the ugliness; his stomach followed from our first taste of what we imagined (not without some previous justification) to be staple Welsh fare—baked beans (in rich tomato sauce) with fried eggs. We had then tossed up as to who should sleep on a couch and who in the bed. I won. The bedroom upstairs had been painted in part; half the floor was acidulous green. But the bed was comfortable, and the view (if one could overlook Mrs. Williams' house) lovely. There was a small back bedroom (again darkened by the rock behind) and a section of it roughly partitioned off to make a cupboard for, I ascertained later, originally a human deposit. The minister—one minister—had let this cupboard.

In spite of all this, we liked the house, because there were outstanding compensations. For instance, through the frequently swamped scullery we emerged into a backyard giving us privacy in the rocks—a sheer wall of slate, which is a beautiful material thus cut, with mossed crannies and little streams in wet weather. We had but to walk to the end of this yard to see the sea, five or six miles away (in a direct line). Then, though the house was immediately saddening, it nevertheless retained a personality likeable and—to employ a word I shall increasingly have to use in writing of Wales and the Welsh in these parts— *pure*. Not just (or here, even) clean—but the quality of never having been dirty. Not pristine, which offers the chiaroscuros of mortality, but of immediate and constant virginity, when virginity is not an ideal of death-addicts. Or virginity is perhaps a bad word, since it is latent with its transformation, whereas Wales is not. Wales is latent with what it *is*—pure, a cleanliness which is not a surface washed but a surface, to repeat, that has never been dirtied. I should qualify *North* Wales.

Then again, though the last resident had obviously expressed her sadness in her indoor environment, the general ensemble nevertheless was of our (anti-Establishment) kind: a gypsy encampment, blessed, in spite of its damp colour, with functionalism, and even reaching out to decoration, which is functionalism beginning to sing. It had a quality of being 'anywhere'; if I loathe anything, it is the excessive and bonding location expressed in the term 'somewhere'. Our friend was in our kind, and her establishment partook of the same; we are a rather wandering kind, and becoming more numerous and—to our surprise —also more topical.

The first human compensation was Mr. Morgan the builder, whose wife is the schoolteacher. He was the first Croesorian to whom we spoke, and the first to provide us with a working conception of what to expect from others: though it must be stated that the villagers are quite extraordinarily individuated. I can think of no two who are alike, in spite of a wide inter-marital relationship running through the whole population (of about fifty people).

Mr. Morgan is dark and slight in build, with large and very soft blue eyes and a very gentle voice. His most noticeable quality can only be called (in no derogatory sense) childishness. I mean he looks like an infant, without this being grotesque. His politeness is wonderful, his delicacy more so, and his tenuous private thought behind his words (he has subtly exploratory eyes) glimmers softly in their depths. His movements have the quick elegance that we quickly learned to regard as a Welsh characteristic—the English move 'with weight'. We later learned that he was quite wonderful in the gentle technique he had of informing us of possible postponement of work to be done. This is not to suggest that the reasons weren't valid; merely that the expertise with which he broadly described the situation compelled one, from its very felicities, to doubt its validity. But deeper than all this (wings of the bird) is his look of absolute integration in his race. He would regard a foreigner (me) with a discreet, a veiled, curiosity (and amusement, I think) of which he was in complete command because he had an interior national H.Q. to whom to make his reports valuable. As a rabbit staring at one from a hillside so belongs to the hills, so does Mr. Morgan to Wales (which suggests he may have Irish blood). Furthermore, like most Welshmen—but more than most—his independence is not in the least geared to the need for any kind of class-aggression or class-consciousness. Perhaps subtle assessments of income take the place of this; whatever does, I am still too much of a foreigner to venture an analysis of what constitutes the grades in the Welsh social hierarchy —certainly something close to talent, of what kind I don't know.

Mr. Morgan, then, like a descended angel, alighted silently at our doorstep for something to do with the water system, I believe, which he adjusted. He was quickly gone, but left with us an impression of delicacy not to be destroyed by encounters with other people of Croesor.

Then we sent the brooms and paintbrushes dancing through the little house, erasing the browns wherever we could. We had very little money, too little even for sufficient paint and none for new furniture. The extreme economicalness of our life had its uses for me, though N—— could have dispensed with it. Deprived of my mild debauches in London, in both rich food and alcohol, my senses were slowly relieved

of that coating of jadedness that a regimen of stimulants imposes. First
the world lurched into desolating space, and silence became alive, as
my ears discharged blocks constructed in resistance to the noises of
London, and to those of my own vivacious chatter in that city, wherein
speech may become the narcotic of thought. Like needles with in-
sinuating points, birdcalls and wind-sounds slowly pricked to life the
inner ear which communes directly with the brain. I resumed intercourse with the tonic world. The development and refinement of this
resurrection was later completed by the Welsh voice, about which I
have written below. The effect of hearing on writing is, naturally,
considerable—though not straightforward. Music I have always found
an essential medium of clearance of the litter of undigested sound in
the ear—an external brain contacting the auricular brain. But washing by silence is better than an ear-syringe, because more lasting.
The initial effect on writing is a collapse of patented style and, more
radically, the disintegration of word patterns previously employed
uncritically *en bloc*. Words themselves, entering one's ears to be greeted
inwardly with an indulgent familiarity that precludes their inspection
and savour, and arriving from outside with their advertising matter of
'accepted' meaning to co-operate with this tasteless indiscipline (compelled discipline), became fruitfully unrecognizable for a period;
washed, it isn't too much to say that certain mimetic or calling overtones (not necessarily onomatopoetic) could be usefully *imaginatively*
heard—at the least: further, the muscles of grammar might peer
through their incarceration in 'rules', further modifying accepted sense.
With French as a first language the sound-plasma of English had
always lain heavily on my vocal chords. Stylists whom I admired—D.
H. Lawrence in his poems, T. E. Lawrence in his prose, Manley Hopkins
and Henry James—had intellectually helped to break the plaster of
convention therein; but intellectually is not enough, and my gastric
juices (whose arrival, so faintly but certainly, seems to be a criterion of
personally right writing) could be released only after words had been
washed for me to release my plastic appreciation of them, which is
bound also with their vocative sense. If this process is hurried and
superficed, we have the parody of a native style—so-called *avant-garde*
associationalism and rhetorical sound.

Our poverty was both painful and delicious. Painful because, an endemic alarmist, I live on the assumption that I may not live; N—— lives on the opposite assumption, a degree of optimism capable of frightening me. For some time our sole source of money was the reviewing I did for the *T.L.S.*; nearly fainting with anxiety, I would ultimately be reduced to telephoned enquiries (so that the assistant editor of the *Supplement* sounded like my long-dead mother in his reassurances). Further, I had previously lived as a co-operative 'bread-winner' with my other wife. I now was the sole one; its effect was interesting. It introduced me to—and made me, perhaps with secret grandiloquence, observe—the vulnerability of human beings; I connected a human tremble with the alarm of poverty in someone other than myself. This finally ousted my old-favoured operatic drama that the poor, in lieu of a better, concoct out of economic insecurity. I found my tensile allergy to making money finally abolished; in part because I realized that at my age I was too set in my ways and thought to make even a passable prostitute, but more because I realized, quite finally, that life without money is too impossible to be dramatic. Even, I believe, I began to connect work with life; after all, it was what I cared to do—writing—that had become geared to survival. And for those who are touchy about concentrating on their own survival (for lack of an identifiable beloved) a dependent wife makes a useful pair of shafts to give one the feeling of travel through the cart behind one. Survival is not assumptively sweet to everyone—or at least, its arts and technics are not. It is quite amazing how one does not doubt the survival value of another person. Still, I'd never been a fly-squasher in my childhood; only in my period of esoteric celibacy. I am near enough to sadism to tremble with terror at another's pain; that is all. I know the trait well enough.

So I became out of love with the hammer of fate, and N—— adroitly began to interpose a nail useful to an article of life's furniture between the hammer and it. She seemed to create freedom out of my sentimental fatalism. The Aweful lost its treacle, because I began lapping it up.

N—— came to life for me in this proper setting for her, Croesor, after the initial blaze I had seen in Suffolk. Clarity without tension, cleanliness without the dragon of hygiene, fitted well into the village-world. The lines of her character are as simple as a good Matisse drawing's—but Cocteau (if I remember) sometimes did better. Eyes, upon which I largely live, I assess in value by the degree to which they do not interrupt my gaze into them; ocular identification is a path of my life. Eyes are the world in the human being. N——'s were no obstacle to my travels. Beautiful eyes have always the hint of not focussing, but never in the sense of obscurity; the poet's eyes, by having no fixed focus (which is obsessional), are exclamatorily focussed on anything. I have seen brown pellets in eyes, and several eyes in one. I have even seen flat eyes, which undress one. And there are eyes like ovens, in which one has to avoid being cooked to a turn. There are eyes like forks, too, in which one must look unappetizing for self-protection. Eyes like *knives* and forks (one must be gristle to them), and eyes like pools in rock, like N——'s.

The poverty was many times delicious (for myself, not N——; she was—hopefully—not in need of this sensory therapy). It seems to me to be quite impossible to observe the behaviour induced by private wealth (in its class degrees of incidence) without having been *very* poor, and to the extent of one's poverty outside society. So much of what is called human nature is class nature and economic nature: by no means absolutely distinct from human nature (somewhat of an abstraction still), but also by no means happily integrated into it. And it is in our time, when class shifts have been formidable, the new rich as lively a crop as ever, the fallen bourgeois inclining to new subtleties, and the 'meritocracy' up and coming, that the distinction is so clearly visible; for the 'human' adopts and employs and deploys the social mask and costume. But our early poverty in Croesor, from the circumstances, was not for this function; I had had that before. It was for sensory therapy; cleaning the palate to taste anew. We ate the simplest things, and I began to drink water (here, the best in the world). At one time we had no shillings for the meter, and I made an oil lamp out of a tin with a string of cloth slotted through the lid; its flicker shot the room from clock time and geographical space into some functional laboratory, a cell of reflection; the firelight looked hopeful. We were enclosed in our cell of life for, obviously, a new birth. As the rheumatism immediately following upon the absence of stimulants left me, almost pristine movements flowed; a queer, half-emerged dance. Somehow our *hearts* became candle flames flickering in the economic winds; the heart and money, since money is survival, are closely linked. (As so often, the point of a cynical attack is better expressed as a fact of life.) The heart-flame is a life-flame: the economic wind can blow it out. At imminent extinction its flame tightens close to the wick, and splutters before it reaches a new height, like a tulip—making one rather awful, very serious in the necessary strategies of obtaining more grease. An odd fluency then, too, like living in orchestral percussion. Can one even hear the tom-tom calling 'dark forces' into work? Certainly a lyrically drawn abandon—something festive about all crises, hence their intoxication (my mother couldn't do without them; they're the brandy of the damned). And crises are the best alibis of proper work; my allergy to security is partly my allergy to the work one may do in it. 'High' drama means poor work, as a colourful life tends to the production of colourless prose, and Spain to abstraction. Nevertheless, a crisis like every kind of situation has always its essential meaning to offer; so one may prise apart its phases, name them and know them, reach even to the distillery whence the intoxicant comes. The distillery is but the sealed-off infant insecurity, when an addiction was formed because understanding was precluded. Drop a babe on its head and it may well be tempted, in later life, to throw itself from a cliff edge. Frighten a child and it will frighten its own children, and literally *live* in fear—need fear to make it feel alive: hence the usual failure of propaganda of terror to dissuade people from war. Fear is a general drug. But happiness inspires to unconstitutional inspiration; love being the mother of this intelligence.

We walked in safety in our miniature 'High Street', as safely as in a room. We began to explore the country, some of the most beautiful I have ever seen; and to explore the people.

3

Some People and Landscapes

IF ONE faces the chapel (bravely) from the bridge, Croesor is roughly cruciform. But there are two buildings before the arms of the cross: the school, a Victorian ecclesiastical-style building, and opposite an empty house, a white-plastered and unlovely affair with cherry-red paint on the woodwork. On the right higher up is Mrs. Margaret Williams' house, when we first arrived still a shop. There are then two terraces, the one on the left being a little lower than the one to the right of the chapel. In this first terrace we have, at the end, a house used in the holidays; then, left to right, the houses of Mr. Morgan, Mrs. Jones (post office), Miss Owen ('shocking'-pink wood) and two joined for Mr. Styles, the novelist. We climb a little higher up the street to enter the right-hand terrace. There is first Ty Capel, like a lean-to on the chapel, then Mr. Bob Owen's detached house, and then the row inhabited by Mrs. Jones's sister, someone I don't know next to her, then another holiday house, then Auntie Gwen's. Mr. Emrys Williams' farmhouse, erupting modernity at the lower end of the street, completes all of Croesor proper. The houses are all, as suggested, plain: a matter of design not materials, however, which are local grey stone. The two terraces are in two blocks. Nevertheless, from a distance (such as the sides of the Moelwyn, near to Bryn Hyfryd where we now live) the effect is charming, because the houses are so loosely disposed and thus have every advantage of their setting to ameliorate their architectural harshness. They are Victorian functional, as Le Corbusier's may one day be functional of his period in the same sense—a warning to us not to prevent the song of the functional, organic decoration. (Nothing dates more than the most modern.)

The village itself is sited about 500 feet above sea level and at a distance of about five miles (as the crow flies) from the sea and Portmadoc. Until the early nineteenth century the sea reached the feet of the hills or low mountains upon which Croesor is built, and, for the questionable advantages of rather poor soil salvaged by Madock's dam, much beauty has been lost. (Mr. Styles has published a novel, *Men Against the Sea*, about this.) The dam itself is typical of much engineering design of the period and an undoubted blot on the landscape. Croesor is also at the end of a valley of about a half-mile in extent, bounded on one side by the mountain range dominated by Cnicht (about 2250 feet) and on the other by the Moelwyn (at the top 100 feet higher than Cnicht). In the bed of the valley a small mountain stream runs, providing us with our bathing-pool just behind Bryn Hyfryd. Five or six farms are grouped round about the village, and the total population is about fifty.

Like most new arrivals I resented even newer arrivals (a technique of inhabitation that few can dispense with). But when I began exploring the mountains I at least understood the point of their quest. Behind Croesor, up the 'Roman Road', one meets solitude. The distant Snowdon range and the ridge over which one has climbed form another, much larger, valley; and as one walks towards Cnicht, a smaller and lower range comfortably encloses the wanderer from the world. The country is composed of small, often spongy pasturage for sheep regularly punctuated by protuberances of grey rock. Half-way up this valley is a deserted farmhouse, roofless but of quite large dimensions, far away from any road. Higher up still, below Cnicht, is a gorge through which a cold draught blows, the rock rising steeply on either side. Through this gorge, some way along, is a lake, absolutely humanless, absolutely quiet. I once met two climbers here, but only once. Such solitude is at first enervating: one's huddled self-conception drops off like the chatter composing so much of it; but then it is a bath, a source of expansion to what once must have been normal human personality (such as one may still experience after a period of tramping alone anywhere). I notice my face, because the lack of people makes nervously noticeable its suddenly unemployed expressional mechanisms; follows blindness, into which the mountains, the lake and the sky gradually pour, in a torrent of impersonal vision. The head feels light, being undressed of its sensation of usual mentation. From a crushing insignificance the body achieves a normal existence in untrammelled space; one moves through and away from all the people one has ever known, including one's 'self'. Yet all the while (in early visits) one snatches cravenly at the flying rags of personality; one clings to 'conveniently' mundane sentences in one's mind. In the split seconds when they're gone, one's in a bowl of existence, and dutifully wonders at many mental conveniences so often merely exacerbated into existence by social claustrophobia. Silence is even more peaceful than music. Perhaps we all secrete an allergy to too much humanity, when human beings, for reassurance, insist so markedly upon their existence and their value to each other? How uncertain both must be. Were I a millionaire, I would build the 'great good place' of Henry James for refreshment from our beloved brothers, and it would be here. Peace from humanity can be a major deterrent to war with too much humanity; for one returns cleansed, and the world is brighter for one's temporary absence from it. The *physically* organized therapy of solitude is better, I think, than the commoner religious therapy of the same (the functions of each are, of course, comparable); for the religious requires some hard-worked auto-hypnosis, hard to come by for those of less faith.

I thus had begun to understand another great advantage to be enjoyed by living in a village among villagers; that in a minute one could be clear of them. People from whom one can be free so easily take on a new form and are known in a new way to the town-dweller. For one thing, the strain of perpetual intercourse is not there, and with this goes also the hallucinating over-personalism of such constant intercourse. By this I mean the inevitable phantasies one builds around people whom one has stopped seeing in perspective and upon whom one impinges, who impinge on oneself, in the hallucinatory forms of exaggerated significance. It is odd, therefore, that villagers engage in a degree of personal feuding less noticeable in town, but equally active there (between neighbours, whom to love is so curiously difficult). But villagers rarely go for country walks; perhaps in some traditional pattern of behaviour, pre-urban, they cling to the safe homestead and

The author with Margaret Williams

Ben and Dafydd Croesor Bach

its environs. So in Croesor an impressioned Garden of Eden slowly crystallized into congeries of alliances and hostilities. As though to compensate for the lack of material in a small community, one person in the eye of another assumes huge proportions; sometimes, against a mountain background, this creation acquired the attributes of a phantastic reality in my own eye. But as outsiders we were quite spared participation in the wars.

This new view of people occasioned by their simple detachability is primarily an aesthetic one. Because detachability disables the warrior in us (war arising from congestion), we begin to see people in the round. We do not relate their every opinion to our own, and we do not competitively display a characteristic of our own to each one of theirs. We do not think of their blue eyes contemptuously as being not the brown eyes we have or, to bring the matter down to more concretely social levels, we do not experience an inner misgiving at more or less culture, more or less taste, more or less class status. Instead, we regard human beings as related to us in the only worthwhile manner: as fellow existences with differing ideas with whom communication may or may not be mutually beneficial. (In a village such an attitude is safe; there are no enemies of society to be found—in Croesor, anyway.) Hence, once we see them in a sufficient space, the necessary context in which to see human beings, they become animated still-lives for a while (this is the view of them as epileptic centipedes having their deserved rest). They may be studied (in the relaxation afforded by non-competitive discussion), walked around and withdrawn from for gestation of the results. Of course you may say an error is already there in such a view; I am proposing a Robinson Crusoe view of men, having mystically detached them from their social and class contexts. To an extent this is true. But the class situation is not what it was. I don't mean that class alignments have ceased to matter, but that the grades are still mobile after the immense shifts since the war; that the English, in a manner typical of either their genius or their folly (the two are probably identical), have stolen a class conception from Marx and made of it something as serious as an Emmet railway or a Betjeman poem. They have transmuted class into a glass of fashion, something worn, a branch of haute couture. While this is going on,

D

as it still is, one may excusably retire (for a while) from considering the matter at all. Therefore a view of people outside the usual class concerns can be refreshing; this is especially true of Wales, where social class has a rather different appearance to that in England. Manners are, for instance, of an almost American democratic ease; I think the real divide is much more strictly economic, and that can find no possible expression (short of murder) in the manners of so volatile a people.

Hence a common existence may suffice as the human bond in Croesor; this says very much less than it may mean. The landscape ordains permission to every aspect of every character; the Chapel may intone contrariwise, but the Chapel is well dealt with by the Welsh. It is put in its place, which is not utterly unconfined, since human beings are naturally allergic to total petrification. The Welsh are more than most allergic to suffering this apotheosis of conventional virtue; they have, I sometimes think, nearly identified sin with life: at least, the battle between this conception and that of virtue as life is more spectacularly joined than it is in England, where life was long ago seen (thought to have been seen?) to be neither, but a grey compromise meaning nothing. Here virtue tends to thunder, but wickedness tends to sing; both are impressive in their different ways. Or does song carry them out of both categories? Sometimes—when it is very good.

But to return to the people; we must first have a clear conception of the Welsh voice, because it is an essentially characteristic one, and it means as much as one has the energy and the ability to discover. The voice is the call of the soul, and is everywhere inhabited by a quality of song, muted or expressed, which (were we given sufficient auditory intelligence) explicitly states the regional 'philosophy'—the path of racial emergence from primitivism, the kind of path and the kind of goal implicitly or explicitly envisaged—before this racial character has become ameliorated into nationalism and internationalism. (It is a sad experience to hear the song in a child's voice becoming furnished into the prose of reasonable speech . . . musically sad, I mean.)

The voice is a vocally sculpted call; the vocal sculpture (or expressive modification) is characteristic of the society into which the call is trained, of the purposes it is called upon to have. A call is desire, primarily, then protest; in the confines of a city it quickly becomes either piercing or a statement. But in a mountainous country its natural quality is retained to carry simply over great distances, and to be refreshed and encouraged by mountain echo. The Welsh have not lost the call in their voices; singing is but a more intense use of it to them, without a change in kind. It fills the ear as well and completely as the Russian singing voice; it washes it. So the Welsh voice penetrates by wooing, because song evokes an infinitely more profound response than speech, which tickles the brain and can only draw it in poetry. Croesor speech penetrates to a new seat of responses. Millions in London have achieved a generalized voice, within the limited class categories. Croesor speech is particularized in kind, and then individuated within the kind to an extraordinary degree. The volume is greater in each individual voice, but because the articulation is very clear, very beautiful, this is unnoticeable. The vowels are clearly comparable to the ovoid sounds of the river over the stones; the consonants are succinct, properly exploited in their lapidary integrity for the intonation of the vowels. The image for a word here is a stone-ringed mountain pool, the water being the vowel. Moreover, one consonant is like the scraping of one stone over another: several inhabitants have a guttural 'r', exactly like that of the northern French. The net effect of hearing such speech is the loss of that impressionistic pressure of inhibitory sensitivity that may describe the indirectness of expression in London speech. The heart and brain, by immediate sensory contact (clear hearing induced by clear speech), are immediately provoked to expression: people are nearer in speech. Hence an immense amount of it is done; one might even suggest an auricular community to compensate for lack, where there is lack, of the other kind. Hence the peak of community in Wales is found in song, and great heights in speech; the silent Welshman is the unhappy one. Hence the popularity of gossip also—an incipient kind of anthropology by the vicarious living of other people's sinful lives. Curiosity, prying, inquisitiveness, have their ultimate uses in a battle against privacy which I, for one, approve—though the immediate results may be painful. The neighbour peering behind lace curtains is but a shy student of mankind. The Welsh are very studious, and never without their staple diet of the sins of others. I am quite as curious as they, but lack the pleasures provided by a strict conception of sin.

When I had first visited Croesor with Denis, the first person I spoke to was Mrs. Margaret Williams, then of the shop. She looked wild to me then: a long sallow face, a long nose and firm chin, slightly hooded eyes that appeared to look in two groups of several; such penetrating, information-extracting eyes. She had then but glanced at me when, outside her door, she had pointed to the chapel and said: 'That's where the hypocrites go!' But she has now joined their number to discover, I'm sure, that her assessment was too sweeping (for hypocrisy is the least of the matter, and ritualized idealism the most).

Mrs. Williams is primarily a worker on a titanic scale. As an afterthought, she was at that time a shopkeeper, but appeared to disapprove of making profit; there, she kept her virtue unimpaired, and the shop closed next year. She is a widow with five children, four of whom live with her. In summer she may often be seen with a line of children following her about the village; not content with her own, she collects a variety of other people's to look after. She is firm but popular with them; her strong physique and a certain positive calmness they find reassuring. In her one may realize the extraordinary quickness of response of these people; whereas a lifetime may intervene between question and reply in Suffolk, Mrs. Williams has rolling behind her like a goods train innumerable responses from which she casually selects the most suitable; if she is mistaken, before one is aware of it there's another in its place. Her technique of becoming informed is superb. She never asks, but brushes the incipient idea of an offering from her interlocutor to excited expression by the briefest and most glimpsing of references. She reduces one to an agony of wanting to impart information, a technique only slightly marred by her intense pleasure in talking herself, which must have caused her to miss many a titbit. In a word, she is rather more sociable than Croesor can quite provide the amenities for; though much is done, with the high street as an external parlour. Conversation it must in part have been that made her business career so brief; sometimes one forgot to ask for what one came to buy. She had also a habit of not recommending her goods. To parry her stream of conversation is extremely difficult; one looks for an opening as China's enemies must have looked at the Great Wall; should she overhear but the subtlest attempt at shifting a brick, reinforcements are rushed to the rescue. The technique of drawing matters to a close I later began—but didn't positively succeed in perfecting—to discover. It is done by studying her rhythms and breathing; one learns to breathe and emulate the rhythm and then, smartly, to catch the first silence with a word in her own rhythm. This has the effect of making her feel she said it herself, and thereby accept it. Her technique of *starting* a conversation is without rival; she will usually look positively unwilling to talk; so one says something, to which she says more. The ends of conversation may endure from her doorstep until, at a distance, one feels able to stop the twistings round for last words that have reached for a long way down the road. Since I had been a non-stop talker myself in my more vigorous youth, I had no principle upon which to resist her. Besides, I am usually interested in all she has to say; the journey may be long, but there are many places of interest.

I think one explanation of her phenomenal dedication to talking is that she is, in appearance and mentality, a 'public' woman. She would have done well in the radical wing of a town council, for instance; her urge to talk is in part that horror of privacy that some people have (as I have)—an unconscious sense of the hygiene of keeping nothing private, which is considered so shameless in England and in most places. It is that she tries to interpret into public speech her every thought. Most people spend as much energy in keeping things back, to the loss of the world. Moreover, her education. (she was once a schoolmistress) has slowed down her native Welsh reflexes and thereby created a sense of distance between thought and speech and between impression and expression, especially of course when she speaks English (I suppose, the 'educated' speech of Wales). English on the whole very much slows down Welsh reflexes, and seems temperamentally unsuitable to them. (Dylan Thomas found the way out of this in rhetoric, the most static kind of expression.) In the past she might have been a witch, and in the future a Minister for Home Affairs. She has a fund of kindliness, but also, sometimes peering through this, what I can describe only as a witch quality—which is what? A scepticism so brilliant of human fallibility and human poverty and unreliability of expression, and sincerity, as to be semi-conscious, unavailable to the thinking consciousness. Gypsy eyes have it, and so have Jewish eyes; and many Welsh eyes. It embarrasses the plumply souled; it is, in the eye, like a feather of razor hairs, the sharpest glance an eye may have. Mrs. Williams has this; it sometimes erupts in wild humour, a little larger than Croesor. She once held up a red vegetable from her garden and, with quite surrealist abandon, called 'Bloody Mary!' over the garden wall.

N—— very quickly struck up a friendship with Mrs. Williams, chattering like a small stream accompanying a deep river to the seas of matrimonial *sagesse*. She must have gained much confidence from Mrs. Williams for the consolidation of what might have been a rather wild adventure into a decorous alliance. On the young face I observed, like history in the making, the fine drawing of new lines of authority and percipience; observed tentative gestures become firm and, in a matter of months, woman emerging out of girl. In the fields and on the mountainsides the lambing season was beginning, the daffodils were out, the buds pressing, and the river flying by with a tenor song after the bass of the winter floods: skies, so noticeable here and so near, were lightly mottled with bits of sunny cloud, for it was a very beautiful springtime that year. Another use of the country is the beatific coincidence of its moods and rhythms with the personal.

Behind Ty Capel was a small plateau with three little trees, where we took tea when the sun shone. From a minutely delineated fragrance we could see the sea and the mountains over the village roofs, perched high up in the fine air; *positive* peace is fully furnished with the world's things.

4

Minds, Bodies and the Chapel

MENS SANA IN CORPORE SANO has amused my generation because
health in bodies had been established by our parents—or by theirs
rather—to mean ascetic; the 'sound' mind springing from that
exercise, appropriately enough, to mean conformist. Viewed otherwise, however, the tag advises sensibly. One casualty of the Victorian
meaning was the later implicit denigration of physical health, even in
the conventional sense; the queer Nazi respect for it, glamorizing
publicity of it, seemed to justify (at least for intellectuals) the
reactionary nature of good health. For over a century some of the
best and most perceptive writers appeared to have extracted their
powers at the expense of their bodies; it was not considered that
they may have had a good foundation to sustain such experimental
depredations. Obviously the body to Baudelaire, Rimbaud, Verlaine
and others became conceptually the symbol of orthodoxy: which it
was, because their earliest conditioning had been orthodox. By attacking orthodoxy in the representations of their infantilely conditioned
bodies they but served to demonstrate a truth so unwillingly received
by a metaphysically orientated society, that body and mind are one. But
we would be foolish to discount, because of this, the value of experiment in the refinements of perception upon the basis of their imagined
separateness. Our knowledge of body/mind unity or identity can, however, put such experiments in their place, which is an important one.

It is one part of the body, conceptually dressed as 'mind', that
attacks the other part, conceptually dressed as 'body'; the mental
derangement resulting from thoroughgoing asceticism and disguised
in the general compromise is psychosomatic, in which specifically

sexual aberrations are found both to have conduced to and been causative of such 'mental' aberrations. Wilhelm Reich, who on his Freudian basis was the pioneer of such discoveries (D. H. Lawrence had his poetic insight thereupon), has never been published here to spoil wicked innocence (Herbert Read tried much to have Reich published in England years ago). In our world we have a shared insanity, so that individual insanity may wear the expression of having been incipient sanity, and failed. The insane include those who took the departmentalization of the individual with a Schweickian literalness.

That the conceptualized body is still the seat of orthodox reactions is evident in our schools; the first sign of intelligence, which is always subversive, is a lack of interest in games. In my training college, when I was misguidedly trying to be a teacher, they attempted to persuade me otherwise; their rhetoric was vigorous. But one may foresee the time when an interest in games will be the first sign of intelligence, which will then also be subversive. It is the creative bias to which one attaches oneself; 'body' and 'mind' are important details, are ideological symbols in themselves.

As a body/mind separationist, an incurable one, I can only appreciate the possibilities offered by the end of the historical dichotomy. But I have been at varying distances from the emulation of a desirable unity; in my own small way, playing safe with a peasant instinct, I have dabbled in madness, and am acquainted with the states of being grandly described as those of 'pure mind' or 'pure psychism' by amateurs in the stalls of this unhappy theatre. That what we call spiritual dominion is pure insanity I have not the slightest doubt, both experientially and intellectually. Our increasing social practice (as usual leaving our philosophy and even our science behind) has been to accept this—pragmatically. We are on the way, for instance, to seeing punishment as no longer being of therapeutic value; this is an admission of the immense conditioning factors in life, a corollary of the awareness of the identity of body and mind. Individual will, that psychic elephantiasis, is toppling thereby. In a word, our barbaric conceptions of impregnable individualism are being modified, at the speed of a tortoise outing.

It is with these matters in mind that we find a major use of the country; the relaxation it induces allows mind and the coruscated sense of self to ease gently down into the bathwater of the body-concept which is, of course, pretty hot from its past usage of being boiled to send steam up to make 'mind' and 'self'. Mind is warmed and body cooled when the former sits down again in the latter. And—as we do to the community, so does mind do to body: we rise from the body and the community together. A passionate belief in mental dominion (in the dichotomous sense) goes with a feudal or aristocratic society. Democracy is working compromise, and socialism is for union. Attitudes to sex are the gauge of these activities.

That I should be in Croesor, in 'Chapel-ridden' Wales, next to the chapel itself, thinking of these things was, obviously, nice. Wales may be Chapel-ridden, but there is a powerful horse beneath this rider: he will never be subdued, because he will never be killed. Religion in Wales is an art. Religion is, in any case, the organization of a conflict; its victory would be its death, concurrent with that of the religious. For a long time it has been for most people little more than a hat, decked with psychic flowers; these flowers may, to the odd traveller in their vicinity, wink gruesomely but humorously; 'we grew,' they leer, 'in no *terrestrial* field'. Indeed not. They grew in the safe kitchen-garden department of a pathological one. Yet, as I wish to point out when we encounter the Chapel and its works more closely, it would be foolish to dismiss as pure waste the exercises provided by the Chapel. However, enclosed in premises hardly reminiscent of a sunny meadow, there is an ideal at work; and there is singing of incomparable beauty. To 'have' religion must be the ambition of every true hedonist and voluptuary; better than drink, better than opium, better than art, it provides the great fairway out of this world: and isn't that the ambition of all our sensitive if not over-intelligent art workers? Or of most? Its poetry is sublime; so poetry is losing its standing.

The ideal at work is my enemy in its parts, yet not quite in its direction; that it cannot triumph allows us to concentrate on its virtues, which are considerable. All roads of escape are instructive, because all such roads lead back to an enlarged world. The degree of their circular promenade is integrally bound up with the expansion of the society they attempt to escape.

In Wales one might reasonably expect, from the prevalence of chapels and their good attendances, and from what one knows of Welsh Methodism, a strong ascetic tendency to exist. Quite the opposite is pleasantly the case, at least in Croesor: there is no reason to suppose that Croesor is unusual here. We must of course remember that Methodism came to Wales in 'difficult' times of popular unrest. Howell Harris, largely responsible for its introduction, provides in his own life a good example of some of the uses of Welsh Methodism. The Rev. M. H. Jones, in his bibliographical study of the *Trevecka Letters*, writes approvingly: 'That Howell Harris should have proved himself to be a true patriot and a loyal citizen enhances rather than diminishes his reputation as a leader of men; and the years 1760–3, instead of being a blank in the story of Methodism, were, after all, productive of good results.' Howell Harris enlisted in the English army to save England from 'the Scotch Pretender and from Roman Catholic France'. Methodism in Wales has spent much energy in preaching toleration of the 'oppressor' (and of the industrial boss). That may have been as far as it could effectively go in its advocacy of the subjugation of (Welsh) flesh. 'The soldier in Howell Harris did not obscure the evangelist', writes the ingenuous Rev. Jones; it would be an odd kind of religion, dangerously near to Christianity, that did. The general effect of Welsh Methodism, as of all demotic religions, was to make of the real world a metaphor, to obscure political and economic issues thereby, and, in this particular instance, to strengthen the English rule. But Welsh Methodism is not Welsh Methodists. These must remain, in their individual ways, human. It may well be that the very seriousness of its political and social purposes made Welsh Methodism less successful in the other conventional work of religion—world-renunciation in the ascetic and ethical sense. Certainly it seems to me that the Welsh wear it, as suggested, like a quite comfortable hat, not at all difficult to take off.

Listening, as we did, enthralled, to the volume of sound from the chapel during the three Sunday services, we could not help appreciating the histrionic genius of some preachers in their condemnation of 'vice', mainly (we supposed) the pleasures of reproduction. But these pleasures are very dear to the Welsh, which is a proof of their sanity.

As lovers they have a high reputation, which I feel sure must be deserved. Moreover, their movements are those of sexually liberated people—light, rhythmical, sinuous; their singing, above all, cannot be achieved on an ascetic regimen. No. The Welsh have come to terms with their religion; their Church gives 'vice' splendidly glamorous colours by its glowing anathemas, making it the most wonderful experience for all true worshippers. Many a man would be a saint had he not had the sense of sin to lead him in the other direction. If sin is made the wrapping of 'vice', the delights of 'vice' will, naturally, invest the wrapping. Some, indeed, find the wrapping alone a sufficient meal; they would often be poets. Welsh hymns, sung at their best, are what? Ascetic? On the contrary: they are a celebration of the joys of life—unlike certain Anglican performances, imbued with the very spirit of suburban misery. Welsh Methodism, in this, has much in common with the Roman Catholic Church; paganism at the root. And this celebration of earthly life's joys are directed at a conception of a better world that is only formally dressed as 'Heaven'. The validity of the idealist drive remains the religious symbolization of a social ideal. The only—immense—obstacle is the symbolization.

Therefore, whatever one may have supposed, minds and bodies in Croesor have a relatively happy association in the sense of their dichotomy having developed less than among the English. That the mind suffers from the lack of a full contemporary culture cannot be denied; this lack makes, or keeps, the Welsh mind at its best as an intuitive tool. From my very small acquaintance with contemporary Welsh writing (and then only in translation) I should say that it suffers from cliché and from rhetoric—with, of course, outstanding exceptions. That rhetoric should be the weakness of a nation so nostalgic about its own past and so discontented with its present is reasonable. But the advantage of a relative (living) cultural unemployment is that the mind in Wales has not gone far from the body; when it expresses more spontaneously, we find a quality of lyrical imagination like the Irish at its best. I think the formalized obscurities of Dylan Thomas's verse are in part due to the percussive undertone of true Welsh to his British orchestration. His vitality and imaginative daring were Welsh, and productive of his immense metaphorical fertility—indeed, of his over-metaphoricization in a rational strait-jacket. Had he, in a Welsh living tradition, been a Welsh poet, that might have been to the advantage of his work—and, incidentally, of himself. He would not have been a Celtic sacrifice to the Philistines. But he remained a provincial from a country condemned to a provincial status; hence, the big world confused him, and he became for sale. His mind—and he was an exceptionally intelligent man—became his chief enemy: fitting well into the English romantic sophistry that a poet need not think; of all people a poet needs to think most. When Dylan heard the word 'mind' he saw the monster Intellect, and had a drink. Too much Welsh talent is condemned to scholarship.

With the chapel, the facial expression of the building in Croesor being quite ambiguous (and quite stupid), the general atmosphere of the place is permissive. The righteous may rent at the cost of three Sunday services a brief plinth of moral superiority, but it is never too high above human ground level for them sociably to climb down, and even to live down, once assured of their plinth. Gossip, that artistic tasting of the lives of others, is but overtly moralistic; it is sensibly dramatic. So, as a refuge Croesor is not a place abnormally closed in like a monastery; it is nearer to being another world, unbelievably unrelated to English city life. It is wide open: there is no ultimately possible immunity for the inhabitants from mountains, air and sea; and we do not yet realize the power of environment upon the most secret crannies of the soul, which is perhaps why the world is so ugly.

As a refuge, to repeat, it is perfect in that it is an escape into life of a pristine kind, from the vivacious mortuaries of the city. Every generation has its fugitives; I was brought up by a fugitive from the First World War generation, indoctrinated before I could object into the same outlook. Showell Styles, the novelist, though hardly old enough to be my father, yet more truly belongs to the generation previous to mine of fugitives—both meet, of course. We first saw him being fit, an activity to which I have always been allergic (though something I've discreetly practised without admitting it). He was, I thought, a Boy Scout type; so he may be. A pleasure of growing up slowly is that one cleans old categories periodically, as one learns to find supports for one's moral equanimity other than those of other people's alleged deficiencies; the imperfections of others are a poor and acidulating diet. Here, then, was Mr. Styles conforming to the Boy Scout English type which I'd always kept well clear of. But what's the essence of this type (in its vintage development)? A naive idealism; an unscientific but gallant attempt at the sound mind in the sound body; development of a social sense that could equally wear social-st or fascist forms; a childlike ideal of self-reliance, which anyway may be useful, if apocryphal in its hopes. A worship of 'decency', England's gift to world morality. And decency? The best that can be managed in lieu of true communal morality—too self-containing, too inevitably manneristic: yet workmanlike in its accommodations to present-day reality (or yesterday's—the quality grows in one's esteem by its increasing scarcity). A man incarcerated in this childhood dream is indeed apt to be imprisoned; a very esoteric ideal awaits him, because the decency being absent, the self-reliance being discovered to be apocryphal and unreal, the social sense still an ideal, a very private god is needed to minister to so many wounds.

But Mr. Styles has managed exemplarily. He came to Croesor, he said in our broadcast of that name, because he thought civilization had left the cities. Civilization, he said, is the 'successful finding of happiness through a method of living together, in a community'. In so far as one finds what one wants, he has found it here. An intensely shy man, he is, for me, a novel kind of nonconformist. His manners are very English, his speech very understating and radically modest. Non-conformists of his kind are far lonelier, even more delicate, than the contemporary mass eruption (towards a new conformity). Their nonconformism is closely tied up with what's called neurosis—'neurosis' when the protest doesn't come off, 'originality' when it does: for our witch-doctors persist in regarding anyone's inability to adapt to our crude society as a sign of mental unhealth—it being, of course, the opposite. Such as Mr. Styles have a deep horror of discord and violent competition; they are essentially peaceful people, and they find current ethics too near those of war. When they revolted it was less a matter of sensationally changing behavioural manners than a matter of spiritual adventure: the thirties, apart from the communist movement, were crammed with such prospectuses to new worlds, mainly within. Such as Mr. Styles had advantages as well as the relative solitudes of pioneers. They lacked the popular acceptance accorded to our present enthusiastic misfits—who will be given, perhaps too soon, the price of their conformism. Their revolt was individual and scattered, their ethos largely expressed by the Georgian poets of the early first-war years. As they grew older they became the guardians of the last fragmented pool of what we may call the English soul—to the class of its guardianship, an uncommercial treasure of still Chaucerian brightness and candour. The soul is fringed by a successful screen of convention: foreign gales more than inquisitive neighbours may rustle the screen aside for a view of the very innocent true blue. The pool, the candour and the naivety are in his eyes. He must when very young have bathed in it, been taken away, and at the end of a long road found a safe place of it here, in Croesor: would this soul be the Celtic element in Englishmen? Possibly: if one accepts the soul as the unemployed essence of a person, which can therefore come down in the inheritance of *un*acquired characteristics.

For eleven years, from the age of sixteen, he worked as a clerk in a Manchester bank—unwillingly. In 1935 he left it for ever, and with £32 began a six months' tramp through Europe. Home again, he began writing for various periodicals, including *Punch*. On the outbreak of the last war he joined the Merchant Navy as a gun-layer and spent the most enjoyable time of his life. He hates fighting and would have been a conscientious objector if the war had been other than an anti-fascist one. When he left he held a commission, which gave him less pleasure than his service with the crew. He then began writing in three modes—detective stories, juveniles and historical novels—and is now completing his fiftieth book. He told me he had at one time been at the crossroads of two kinds of work—the artistic and his own, for which he claims little or no such values. Yet his books have a poetry, that of action; that is, the mathematic of such a potential poetry, the lyrical permutations of action (John Buchan, etc.). They do not stand for 'literature' their author agrees—chiefly because the action and the character and ethos run all three parallel to one another, instead of in that mutually affective integration resulting in what we call art. Yet we may find in his *Men Against the Sea*, already mentioned in connec-

ion with Madock's dam, hints both of the Gothic and T. E.
Lawrence heroism of inhibition so general to the generation broken by
the First World War. It is odd to find in so allegedly popular a novel
a hero so Nietzscheanly 'dark', and descriptions of landscape so
Freudianly symbolical in their Gothic dressing. Oddly enough (or
not, in view of the author's happy days on deck), the manservant in
the story achieves most humanity; decency corrupts most other
characters to their histrionic paralysis.

The simplicity of his books is in his face, and, possibly, rather a
superficial simplicity—more likely, a simplification. There's a radiant
quality (in his pretty daughters, also) which is, all the same, something
in front of something else. But his old passion, in which he still indulges, is mountaineering—he has climbed in the Himalayas and north
of the Arctic Circle. I suspect the soul is mostly in his mountaineering
books.

It was the pattern of his life that I especially admired, as soon as
glimpsed it: he has everything, without being tremendously rich. He
has peace, a family, a garden, work he likes, excellent health, and
unquenched enthusiasm for life. He has also methodically tidied up
any regrets he may in the past have had; beneath the sunny smile is
a craftsman's well-jointed philosophy of existence. That this should be
happening in Croesor was encouraging. It had really not occurred to
me that one could be happy without having some major ailment—
criminality, idiocy, for instance. It occurs to few people today—to few
intellectuals, anyway, whose eager acceptance of the burden of the
world seems so admirable from a distance, and a little complacent in
nearer view. Personal misery does not alleviate that of the world,
however; one may think, perhaps, without frowning. And—good
works that are not a development in egoism are ineffectual—so I
believe . . . without the engines of sainthood (but saints are no
exception).

All the people of Croesor have a quality in common, and all of
them are extraordinarily individuated from that common central
quality. The quality is the flower of the particular community in its
particular setting, and it must be called purity—a lack of socially
strategical contriving, an untroubled centre, a ventilation by scenery

and by the fact of the absence of civic cerebral competitiveness. Bob
Owen, of whom more later, has it radiantly; Auntie Gwen, who 'does'
for Mr. Styles, and does many other things as well, has it discreetly,
like an underground stream surfacing in her eyes. Should you have
seen flowers dipping occasionally in a mountain stream from its banks
you will have seen the character of those eyes and also the rhythm,
desultory and continuous, delicate and humming, like stream and
flowers. Her eyes of an unmatched purity, to the foreigner breath-
taking in the first impact: as though, expecting to see a person (an
armoured one, I mean thereby), you found yourself instead gazing
soul-first into the clearest and deepest of pools—not dark blue, but lit
fair by the sky, with passing airs over them. They're utterly impersonal
yet personally kind, like benevolence from an unknown altitude. But
her face is lean and disconcertingly muscular; but to call her ceaseless
monologue 'artless' would be erroneous; because her eyes collect and
store every nuance of reaction in you, by the currents of which she
adeptly steers her light craft—you may not put many words aboard
she implies. She is also inscrutably funny; it would take many years
of knowing her to discover what precisely does stir her wide sense of
humour.

In general, it is the virginal sense of humour at the heterosexual
majesty of other people's movements and ways: her lightness makes
you very conscious of these in yourself. But the bed of her conversa-
tional river will grate every now and then—her face's Judy-like
muscularity warns of stubbornness, and it would be quite silly to
disagree with whatever she does, in the face of her wide provenance
for such possible, and thereby aborted, disagreement. Her singsong
voice intones an unfathomable scepticism of everything she or anyone
says; such scepticism as to have achieved the maturity of a kindly smile
and unfailing simplicity. Her humour is discerned as summer lightning
in her eyes, and grass-fine flickers of the corners of her mouth. She is
not old but ageless. Her general demeanour is mercurial, a born
messenger of what 'they say', with sufficient unwillingness to disburse
what you reactively ache to hear. She distributes news impartially
professionally; she is quite anti-dramatic, and a great relief from our
moving times. When I speak to her her eyes work into mine like

forceps seizing whatever I am unwilling to say, which is also a relief, since nothing is more tedious than one's own impenetrability. Auntie Gwen is the executive body of the village, the *sine qua non* of its civic existence. I list later on her eleven or twelve kinds of activity; she dislikes sleeping, considering it an awful waste of time, and has been seen cleaning the school at two in the morning after conversations more entertaining than usual.

5

Nature, Song and Birth

MISANTHROPY is a conclusion reached from unfounded ideals; it is usual to describe people as a mixture of 'good and bad', and to move away from the great moral generalizations of our forefathers; this is a step towards the inevitable conclusion that the epoch of the *illusion* of individual responsibility in an uncontrolled field—competitive society —is drawing to a close. 'Blaming' makes less and less sense. That, nevertheless, people have a sense of morality is inescapable; its symptomatic character steadily encroaches on its absolutely conative delusion. It is an essential and major factor of ideological conditioning, imbibed so early as to be for ever after religiously regarded. With a wider view we may even exonerate the good from the responsibilities for their actions; they knew no worse. All the same, in all life we can discover pro- and anti-life proclivities; the pro-life would seem to be instinctual, biologically orientated as it is; the anti-life may serve it in primitive circumstances. Unequivocal anti-life is more usefully to be regarded as insanity than as wickedness; the concept 'wicked' is unscientific, belonging to the blackmailing morality of the past, when punishment was considered to have a therapeutic value, whereas therapy has the true punitive value to 'wickedness'. The doctor's punishment of illness is cure.

So in Croesor the mention of one villager to another will produce the classic reactions so often encountered. These are composed of a gathering tenseness, a witch-doctor air of infallibility, and the expressive prosecution of the oldest of wars—of one individual against another. The innocence and intelligence of one is absolutely reliant upon the wickedness and stupidity of another; which, in schools, i

66

still more or less the method of education, and constitutes the ethics of, say, the *Daily Express*.

Moments of parenthetically spectral equality and visioned humanness are moments of embarrassment and of unemployment of 'character', an armament. It is with a sigh that all are, momentarily, agreed to be as good and as bad as all others. The self-conception brightens when deficiencies come again into the hunter's view.

There is a tiredness from the heart when one villager eulogizes another, or else an over-succinctness, an over-positive emphasis that, one sees, means the building of a wall against further speculations that must, in the future, be scaled. Utter agreement makes the beast in us awkward; so we have the moronic adulation of 'controversy' in the daily Press as a virtue in itself, and all the ageing but common epithets of 'hard-hitting', 'forthright', etc., that litter its unpleasant sheets. It is not seen that agreement among peoples is a *dynamic* to adventures; the genius of man in his penetration of Nature is wasted in interpersonal conflict. It is a sign of decadence in England that this conflict should be so admired; Shaw was wise about the House of Commons.

But Croesorians run short of grist even for competitive mills; they are all there, together, near each other in the enfolding mountains; it would take insanity to prosecute with urban intensity whatever feuds there may be. Melancholy may set in among more recalcitrant feuders, like the negative aspect of the mountains.

Utter agreement in the sense of common identity is impossible; insecure identity produces this terror of common identity, and comes to associate individualism with aggression; variety is corrupted into personal competition, which blunts its fine points. Love poured over these ensembles can clog the works, but not alter the machinery. Hence such enjoined love brings life to a standstill, and denudes it of quality. Virtue becomes associated with the static and evil with the dynamic; Lucifer could persuade us of the correctness of this association.

So in Croesor as everywhere sin is excitedly viewed and virtue is liturgically praised. Sin looks like life, though it is but a heady concentrate of it, virtue having lost its vitamins.

It may appear that I have idealized the Croesorians; not so. Because
they lack the opportunities for internecine competition they are gifted
with the (compelled) opportunities for making a community; aided by
the Methodist Church, their driving virtue thus becomes more
substantial than it might be in a town. It may more closely correlate
with their actions—though the strain is considerable. Astounding as it
may be, they 'believe' in it. They believe in the practice of consideration and 'charity'—as we know, a well-tried method of avoiding the
concrete human existence of these qualities—for duty atrophies native
virtue when duty has become a formality. That doesn't make it
entirely negligible, though harmful to the natural character, in so far
as that phoenix has body. To give an idea of the *mélange* of religiously
induced ideal and 'pagan' virtue—and communally induced humane-
ness—one had best try accurately to describe the psychosomatic
adventure of their hymn-singing; it penetrated the walls of Ty Capel
every Sunday with wonderful clarity (as the smoke from our fire was
once alleged to penetrate the chapel).

The beginning of the assembly was, I believe, singing—I'm not
sure. But frequently the address would be given by the visiting
minister. Often, this consisted of a torrent of accusation of human
frailty (we could only judge by the tones; the sense could never have
been as impressive). The speaker would approach song in his anger and
horror of sin; nothing, we opined, could in this world be as formidably
exciting . . . to the minister. And then what, after the digesting
silence? Why, the reply of the *human*, clothed in piety it is true—but
indubitably human. The congregation sang its way out of the morass
described by the preacher. They replied by riding, like shining knights
those horses of 'the passions' that *must* be so passionate in order to
support such riders for such wonderful adventures through the skies.
Their voices called to the furthermost places, terrestrial and cardiac
less sweet than rounded, contained as a cathedral resoundingly contain
voices; and one's breast sympathetically filled with this intoxicating
air, this tonic valiance of adventure. They celebrated the beauty of
virtue, thus making of virtue a substantial way of life; virtue to them
was aesthetically wonderful, a thing both of order and of freedom. It
was positive—all positive: virtue gained her body through the wonder

of their voices, being linked to earth again by beauty. And its energy was pagan, its softness was human, and its highest escarpments religious. Religion here was annealed to life, was become a poem in its celebration; it was riotously happy and put the mess of competition to sleep. Which is why, I thought, the Chapel has no overridingly repressive effect; the very passions its overt ethics condemned were resplendently expressed in its songs. For in what does the blessing of a 'passion' exist? In its aesthetically beautiful expression.

This emotion is the everlasting emotion of humanity, the pointer to better worlds, the *leitmotif* of all proper endeavour; which Wagner whispers. It is the *heroic* and temporary dislocation from the sordid and pseudo-rational, the momentary perspective gained of human struggle for good happiness. No one who hears such song can remain safely misanthropic; it comes in an emotion of invincible power, and wears religion like a bridle. The alternative that religion has given to people of a heavenly bliss, in lieu of an earthly one, has become so formulated, so precise, that the religious comes to yearn for its earthly existence. Once again there is no escape; the engine of escape comes full circle back to its origin. If a man dreams of heaven, he will awake and look for it. So, to reverse Marx, opium is the religion of the people. Positively, it becomes, in Marx's words, 'the sentiment of a heartless world, as it is the spirit of spiritless conditions'. And 'He who has only found a reflexion of himself in the fantastic reality of heaven where he looked for a superman, will no longer be willing to find only the semblance of himself, only the sub-human, where he seeks and ought to find his own reality.'[1]

The dogmas of religion are easily dismissible; they were not rationally propounded in the first place. But the religious emotion is another matter; it is not 'religious' at all, it is profoundly human—the strongest human emotion, an expression of power through brotherhood, with the consequent beauty and poetry of such an awareness. It is, strictly speaking, always revolutionary; once it touches earth, it razes reaction to the ground. Until the socialist movement brings this power to earth, it cannot succeed. In attacking religion, thereby lumping together dogma and emotion, it atrophies its own power.

[1] K. Marx: *Selected Essays*. Trans. H. J. Stenning (L. Parsons).

The dogma fails increasingly to convince in any case; with the emotion 'at a loose end', we get nihilism and despair. The Promethean task has still to be performed.

And Croesor and, to a large extent, the Welsh in general have still this strong emotion alive in them, which in England has been desiccated by industrial ugliness and its 'rational' corollary of petty disillusionment. Hence the lack of art among English socialists, with rare exceptions. (But we have Africo-American music, which still carries the emotion through hiccoughs of embarrassment).

And so Croesor has a rare tranquillity, and is a fine place for children, and for one to be born in; there are about nineteen children in a population of just over fifty.

It has recently been established (in the *Lady Chatterley* case) by a judge that detailed descriptions of those exercises initially responsible for the existence of the judge are not necessarily obscene. This discovery, which goes far to substantiate the long-suspected legality of human existence in general, is also another blow at the cheery doctrine of original sin. It detracts also from the lugubrious mysticism for so long attending the miracle of birth. That birth is less exciting than murder to the majority is clear; I suspect the *frissons* attending the news of murder are not unrelated to the suppression of the excitements attending birth. Human dignity as we know it still consists in shaving off progressively every vestige of nativity; no men look less like having been born than the ornaments of our official life. This accounts for the amusement they cause to intelligent women, and to Thurber. Our officials imaginatively perform the feat of self-conception, where the *double entendre* is apposite. So do most of us. Having lost track of true birth, we concoct our improved version out of which we are splendidly, as personalities, immaculately arrived. I think we would like culture, even principles, to be biologically fecund; this desire has associations with the present popularity of the word 'creative' applied to those who do things with words, paint, stone and, soon to be, who wash the kitchen floor.

In simple women the transition from the usual to the pregnant expression is slight; the usual isn't rodently over-focussed on the ploys of existence, the rhythm isn't cramped; hence there is no spectacular shift in tension. The reader, who may well have experienced being born (after the *Lady Chatterley* case), must remember the gradual cramping of his natural styles and rhythms, the congesting of his tensions from that happy day onward as he became the knowing, able and even brilliant person he is today. This increasing tension is not only ascribable to social exigencies; it is also a condition brought about by our nervous education. Fear may have been modulated to the atmosphere of duty as the means of teaching, but learning is still detached from personal observation and feeling, from the natural brain; knowledge is still loaded, like goods on to a platform, on to a separated public consciousness. Proud the many with a hundred suitcases; that they have lost their keys means nothing, because prestige and efficiency is to do with the having and the traffic of these suitcases, not with their contents, which would include personal pants. Or that every object in each case is felicitously locked inside itself allows the projection on to it of that mysterious essence of reality which is the bride to the careful social disorientation of the groom. Lost generations are the grooms of mystery, and reality becomes forked lightning. To be struck is 'drama'.

One such flash of lightning for men is the pregnancy and delivery of females, situations which evoke from the male some of his favourite emotional operas. His ideological mystification precludes his understanding; his lack of understanding forces a guilt at failure to achieve that substitute for understanding, co-identification with the pregnant woman (in certain savage societies, as is well known, this co-identification is ritualistically enacted). The guilt forces that uneasy opera of feeling so exacerbated by a suspicion of its artifices. Such behaviour is not unlike the orgies of frustrated co-identification that were so common an obstacle to charity-mongers being effectual. The opposite discipline is scientific and human; idealism has made an ocean of crocodiles' tears, in which we all learn to swim to futility.

Fortunately for my tendency to a similar emotional opera N—— took pregnancy as I take food; with competent interest. The middle-class miracle was blessedly absent, giving the understandable wonder a chance. Much of this was due to Croesor, wherein being born didn't appear to be an aberration. Having been responsible for a few pregnancies in my time, I have only on one other occasion been so aware of the normality and the beauty of the events. The beauty is mainly the appearance of timelessness in the woman's features, and the total absence of neurotic fidget in her movements; rhythm becomes plastic. There is the same dancy but un-nervy motion as in the separation of amoeba; a live crystal of pristine motion. That time's chain at last slows down to show us a glittering link is the virtue of it to us. It makes the soul breathe again in its proper expanse, compared with which the world of our daily experience is a cupboard full of history's old clothes. And into this expanse poured the animating, furnishing volume of the singing next door—the celebration of life. 'Character', so much a bruise of our primitive, prehistoric existence, flew away, leaving behind the flower of organic self on which it had perched.

Croesor, like an infant city, is held up by the rock as though on a hand, held half-way up in the air, above the sea, washed in winds to be fit for the sky, and strangely innocent to us during this time. We were in no congeries of opinion or feeling in the village, and N—— has an automatic shaver of adhesive personalism. The priceless gift of the orphan kind is an eye for the unsultry mechanics of human action, as in a Chaplin film. Lyricism of action is born from lack of involvement in tense local issues; and in spite of all the heavy moralia of committedness—in spite of the apparent immorality of this view—such perception is in the long mainstream of human self-regard: it erupts contemporarily in the apologistic form of humour, which comes less from a lack of sympathy than from an extraordinary definiteness of personal contour.

When she was very big with the child, to me like a time-bomb imminently exploding, we went for long walks in the mountains. We favoured a small waterfall beneath which we bathed, where the sound of the fall melted the biscuity discontinuity of anxious thoughts. There again such time, flown out of our anthropocentric distribution, littered the eyes with apparently eternal shapes; that such things might be so always (as far as we were concerned) led us to suppose that we in different forms, with such gradual modifications, might be parts of 'always' too. Out of the scrum such risky 'experiments' revealed their normality; the normality of the world is fundamental peace, whatever tricks we have to get up to to see it, in sheltered parentheses. Life appeared both casual and explicit; as the 'understanding' (projection of beliefs) melted, rocks, flowers and water were revealed. The spectacle was limpid, like the Welsh; one didn't fornicate into understanding with it, and the self was relieved of much sentimentality. How to live with a mass of people without protective and ingrowing opinion has always been beyond me; every thought in a mass is a potential gun, for suicide if one's polite and for murder if one isn't. Where time stops, bliss is born of breathing, a flower for every heart-beat, and the aspect of things is not sublime but something much more profound; it is ordinary. That the ordinary, less and less seen, has by reason of its rare appearance been corrupted to the sublime or the wonderful is sufficient comment on our times. Every Sunday, however, the Welsh 'soul' was undressed to this point of observation; sanity resided in its *highest* reaches, such is our life. But exactitude is the integrity of living, as well as of drawing.

It was then that the hitherto unremarked but now noticeable manner of our reception became evident. It is the fluency of the Welsh (as opposed to the *economic* expression of the English) that accounts for their behaviour with us, and with any foreigner. They see before they know; we know in order not to see the surprising (potentially undesirable). What they see much determines in a straightforward manner their behaviour. Less insulated from happenings, their reactions are lucid and sensible. They appear quick in response, which relatively they are; but this is not from greater mental speed, but from less social inhibition; they are less developed apart, less encased in civic majesty. So when N——'s pains started the matter was public in a way that detracted nothing from its privacy: who really owns flowers? After some wrong numbers the ambulance arrived and we began a drive in Celtic passion to the hospital. The ambulance broke down after two miles but was repaired by another motorist; the driver, on the way back, told me he'd sometimes had to deliver the child himself *en route*, hence his speed and tension. The baby turned out to be a very well-made production (and was never bald). While N—— was in the hospital several villagers (many of whom we hardly knew) sent gifts.

Mr. Morgan drove me all the way to Bangor to see her. In a word, one would have thought that a birth was quite a good thing, and that one person had quite positive associations with others: an enlightening idea to me. I have never so publicly fathered, or even so publicly lived. Since N—— had been reading *Eugenie Grandet*, we christened the baby Eugenie, and added Allaye because we had been reading the *Lost Girl* (Allaye was the lost girl's found name). In spite of this, the child was marvellously peaceful, and continues to be sagely interested in the world and her survival. She is the best eater of her age I have seen. It is because a child, especially a baby, is constitutionally sane, and pulls us to the same sanity, that we are driven 'mad' by its distracting us from our retreat to hermetic insanity by its carry-on. Should we succeed in suppressing it *we* would be orphaned. Two conductors to sanity are there: the peace of Nature and the excitement of children. Before these even the damned soul produces a squirm of life; even the outsider might have a look in.

6

Impending Departure

MY NEW-FOUND peace was still too clearly formulated in my mind
for it to have struck strong roots; when John Jones and his friend from
Manchester (a lecturer at the university, I think) entered at midnight
with a bottle of whisky I watched it seem to totter with a 'ham' leer
of destiny recognized. The leer was ham, however, and the tottering
representative of my nervous new state.

John Jones is what in England would be called a 'gentleman farmer',
Marxist in his orientation and honourable in his looks. Suspicious, I
thought I detected a mystique in his farming life, because he has a
slightly intellectual air, eyes not quite remote from those expressions
of depth-understanding I had learned to dread in London, from a long
acquaintance with fellow conspirators in that 'emptiness of life' that
provokes depth-charges of misanthropic philosophy. I learned later that
he wore the manner easily, and that it was dispensable. A strikingly
handsome man, he seems happy (with a certain aesthetic begrudging
of his happiness; solemn dolour is within reach), and has six attractive
children.

He came to see me, presumably, on a tour of inspection of the
latest addition to the fauna. Inwardly wincing I discharged *en bloc* my
creaking London 'interestingness', inwardly watched the still existence
of this macabre dervish in garrulity. It was like releasing the monkey
within; his friend was familiar, a socially risen person with most of the
now accepted doubts about his status and his integrity. He mulled
over his integrity in the accepted manner, with some dark flowers for
the burial of infant hopes. Under this he was surviving, which was still,
I was glad to see, the chief thing. Yet the lostness of these new merito-

crats is genuine enough, even though (as in *Room at the Top*) its expression is so oddly bogus—because, of course, the road to the alleged damnation is profitably being trod. (Which points to the superiority of Sillitoe: there, any added money and status are organically related to the nearer social origin.) England offers few models other than that of imitation gentlemen to her more intelligent risers in life, which is a great and stultifying pity; it seems impossible to be just a man, or a person. The Manchester man was definitely worried; but operatic, because inconsistently so. The extent of his worrying was evidenced by the positively religious air it cast over his features; the need to feel good is greater, I think, than the need to be good; the times being self-conscious, action is a risk at the expense of sensation. Religion, of course, has always accentuated sedatives of virtuous feelings for the anguish of virtuous actions: the ideal as a carrot is safer than as a meal. Sometimes the Manchester man did a psychic jig at the lovely involvements of his situation; he relished its topicality (just as Herbert Gold in the recent *Noble Savage* wrote that the Beats queued up to buy *Time* in order to find who they were and what they were doing). The Manchester man already existed generously in print, and was torn between admiring his reflection and agitating towards the sensibility of authentic existence. I had an idea that he would get there, if only because we shall have had it, soon, so good. In the centre of his *angst* he was, like most of his kind, childlike; almost evidently waiting for a cue to the next socio-historic move. The drink gradually reduced him to his native cocoon, from which he gesticulated eccentrically: as much of Nature as English weather permits to the more recalcitrant. John Jones did not depart from his safe post of observation of goings-on; after all, he had had his dip into the sea of life some time ago, and had got himself a Marxist boat, sensibly. He had a right to sail on waters where others swam. I, with only a lifebelt, submerged and rose uneasily, watching the urban monkey dancing on his string. For this I got angry with the unwitting organ-grinder, and glared hard at Mr. Jones; he may have been delighted with a symptom fitting into his predetermined diagnosis (one that is usually right in such cases). Nevertheless, he left me with an admiration of as good an example of outer appearance suiting inner principles as I shall see for some time (in the one case in which I met it in the past, a rupture between the two occurred: he now keeps a pub, which is jolly).

When they left, I for a moment saw the new little world smashed, and by emphatic ritual next morning did my *pujah*. The lesson: not to formalize the real—a less arduous exercise than formulating it. Also the experienced propinquity of my two worlds, urban and Croesor, opened to me a perception concretely sensory of their respective differences. What I have written about the cleansing of my senses in Croesor resulted in a continuity of the new reality that made it unconsciously assimilated. But when they had gone the world of clogged senses returned. (I had no reason to doubt the complete inter-affection of mind, senses and world; in the South of France, in the small village where I lived, I once smoked Player's cigarettes; the village went two-dimensional.)

I have met people (preponderantly in the middle-class bohemian fringe) who have 'new lives' every few months; each one lifts them to yet another layer above the increasingly menacing point of departure. Nervous breakdowns are common to new-livers, when they reach too high for nourishing air. Each new life is scooped from the larger context of the old one; in the end, life and the liver are self-conceptually identified; and look out upon the wasteland created by the greed for this sensation of self, this substitute for the world. It is essential, if ever a new life comes one's way, progressively to take down defences against the old; otherwise the old invades and destroys, when the new has become hopelessly formal, abstract and solipsist. D. H. Lawrence lacked this technique; but then the old was such a horror to him. We scramble to emulate the life with which we fail to deal, in a technique of mimesis, like that of primitive magic. Hence the plethora of vital and interesting people; one should approach them with circumspection.

That my conception of Croesor was not phantastical was brought home to me when my friend Annie Lowson came down with her film, for which I was to write the commentary. She sensed the same qualities. She is Danish and has decided that her most self-committing view of life is through a camera; she possesses a good eye for pictures. We worked happily on the commentary. A quality in the film—freshness and straightforwardness—found its support in Croesor.

But our tenure of Ty Capel was reaching its close. Not long before we left we attended an election address by the Welsh Nationalist candidate. Most of Croesor is Welsh Nationalist, though only one or two of them anti-English. *Plaid Cymru* did well in the election, polling over 2000 votes; it is, I believe, the only political party in the British Isles in support of total disarmament and the abandonment of the H-bomb; Wales, even to the dullest intelligence, having nothing to gain from these old-fashioned exercises in 'might'.

The candidate, Mr. Gwyfor Evans, was not at all like most of the political speakers I'd heard. For one thing he didn't talk like a salesman, neither did he dispense detachable charm. Charming he certainly was, and his address one of the most intelligent I've heard at political meetings. He totally lacked cunning, and didn't give the air of burgling our brains for agreement. Instead he gave facts and figures of what English domination of Wales had meant: both cultural and economic impoverishment, he declared. There was also a serious decrease in the Welsh population. (*The Welsh Nation*, organ of *Plaid Cymru*, instances Merioneth as having suffered a 6·7 per cent decrease since 1953—the greatest in England or Wales.) *Plaid Cymru* is evidently on the increase in numbers and influence; *The Welsh Nation* lists it fourth in political parties in England and Wales. Actually the feeling for independence, where it exists, is strong, and not based exclusively on economic factors. The fact is that Welsh culture has never been entirely absorbed by that of the master race, but has been prevented thereby from properly developing. The extraordinary difference between the two peoples should, one would think, have political representation. Without separation, *Plaid Cymru* reasonably enough argues, there cannot be proper co-operation. It shows signs of being a very positive kind of nationalism, imbued not so much with hatred of the English as with love of its past and its own people and culture. It is to be presumed (since the English are against self-rule) that England would lose economically from separation; it should therefore be presumed that the Welsh might gain. That the English have for long delighted in the uses of the territories of other peoples is not of course news; the moral spreads on this appetite have always been quite delightful. One knows that cunning man may be moral about anything; it is a matter of moral organization and nice phrasing; English arrangement of its psyche commands the admiration of all peoples.

Of course, as a non-political tourist, an English subject of Irish and Dutch extraction, I have no national feelings at all; but aesthetic ones are not quite to be detached from politics. It seems to me good that nations should manage their own affairs; without self-rule, internationalism is impossible; for unity is always positively achieved by diversity: it is *proved* therein. Under what is at least regarded as foreign oppression the arts are forced into a narrowly chauvinistic attitude, of Welsh formalism *vis-à-vis* the English variety; organic growth, wherein expression taps the national character and genius, is not possible. The urge for art is immense; the Eisteddfods that take place all the year round in villages and towns, whatever the quality of their productions (of which I have no idea, not being a Welsh speaker), the fact that it is not at all uncommon to find farmers writing poetry (like our David Williams at Croesor Bach), is clear enough evidence. Art and life are very close here, and community feeling is high; the *safety* of the community is no small matter in encouraging art of a kind distinct from that of the sad *avant-garde* (yesterday's and today's) of the rest of Europe.

The Labour candidate was returned, as before; *Plaid Cymru* has dissociated itself from the Labour Party in, it seems, a trend common to many progressive groups. Having consolidated its metaphysic of progress, Labour appears to expand its physical Establishment.

There's no doubt that the Welsh of the North (at least) have retained that 'natural' life so commended by Lawrence, and which psychologists are increasingly suggesting is something one must return to. This is because the Welsh in the North have bypassed the worst horrors of industrialism, and could conceivably take a lead in the next lap of civilized and socialistic construction. The so-modern Englishman, intellectually glittering (if that is not exaggeration), glitters from the dead place, the lacuna left by too much industrial competition; that is to say, he is, as we know him, being bypassed. The new world of co-operation will find his competitive psychology obstructive; the more communally minded Welshman is more truly a modern the making. Oppressed nations have had one wonderful opportunity: to bypass the competitive psychology and in its now anachronistic expressions. Good economics, we know, are co-operative ones; there has not been, and never can be, a good case to put against this universally present, if universally veiled, fact of life. It has the added grace of being ethically Christian. How a Christian could be anything but a socialist I have never understood: it is the lore of lovers.

Blodwen Evans, for instance, is a delightful example of the eccentricity into which ultra-competitiveness is forced in these communal parts. A 'character' *par excellence*, she thrives upon differences. We first met her on a visit to Edith's cottage, Blodwen then living next door. Blodwen stood with some of her brood—perhaps with all of them, about five—arms on hips, looking belligerent with suspicion and sardonic with amusement as we approached. She is a short stout woman with strong hips and a manly chin, one eyelid rather drooping. She was the centre of quite a little feuding in the village, having more than most people with whom she didn't talk. But next time I met her walking to Croesor from Llanfrothen with a filled shopping basket, which I carried. It was then her (inexpressible to me) humour sidled into her boxer's face. Her speaking voice is the most singsong of all the people I have heard here (she was a star attraction in our radio programme because of this voice). She was once the chapel choir's great asset with, I'm told, a superb singing voice. It is a string upon which all her words appear so negligently strung. Having heard that she was slightly given to our favourite occupation here, the discussion of other people's affairs, I was charmed to hear her say that she took no interest in the doings of other people. Having heard rumours of her belligerency—we may call her a magnificent fighter—it was fascinating to hear her sing that she loved everybody, in our broadcast. She mimics and mocks with the fresh discovery in her talent of a child. She is obviously delightfully happy but, as suggested, anachronistically competitive. Not only did she refuse, from some tiff, to shop at Mrs Williams', but even commanded her neighbour Nellie (now our own) likewise to refrain. War was serious to her; she must have planned She was also immensely curious, eating the world through her eyes She could stand and stare immovably; eventually one's own self-regard integrated with hers, to produce embarrassment (the only reason why one resents being stared at). Eventually she left for Pen-rhyndeudraeth, and we moved into her cottage.

We were now become a complete *ménage*, with two adults, a baby, a dog called Monty aged fourteen and a cat Toto, aged a few months but already showing signs of a remarkable appetite. We loaded ourselves into Annie's car and went to Suffolk for the winter, which I knew well from a previous sojourn there.

In Suffolk we found the physical reassurance of a familiar landscape and familiar friends and neighbours; which produced, so interestingly, the insecurity consequent upon a compulsive sociality. Suffolk is the opposite of Merioneth in most things. It is mournful; Wales is not so at all. The Suffolk natives are unbelievably slow of speech; manners are as feudal as anywhere in England, and the gentleman is still an osten-tatious power. The country is also rich in intestinal creators of art; the lugubrious atmosphere makes a friendly setting for European agony, the artistic cure for which, evidently, is more agony. The air is very heavy, the soil very rich; we were struck by the contrast with what should be called, I suppose, the poverty of Wales, and yet which looks not at all like poverty, but like refinement. It is the dearth of spirit and the exaggerated chore of survival that make Suffolk so popular with the professionally disillusioned creators; it passes by the name of realism always, *anglice*, the less unpleasant aspects of life. Our souls dampened appreciably, with the resultant coarsening of our recent happiness. So, after six months, when we heard that Blodwen's cottage was vacant, we wrote to Mr. Williams-Ellis and secured the tenancy. We returned in the spring of 1960, and almost at once got to work on our broadcast.

7

The Broadcast

WE HAD no time to get to know our neighbour Nellie Jones and her children—Raymond, Hefina, Leonard, Valerie and David—before David Thomson arrived. But the recording served as an introduction to the odd dozen people we interviewed. For the most part their responses were much more assured than were my questions. My tentative manner encouraged some comic dialogue, some of it too associational to be quite strictly comprehensible. But *their* lack of self-consciousness was remarkable. They loved communicating. I've always hated and been depressed by reticence and privacy, being most un-English therein. I regard the hermetic characteristics of our so-cherished 'private life' as intellectually most unfruitful; how may one compare lives when so many are sealed off? And if lives are not to be compared and discussed, half their use is gone. I think everything should be thrown into the common pool. But the castle-home attitude is here for a long time; much less so in Wales. That's the positive point about rich and detailed gossip; it but represents an interest called scientific when indulged in by sociologists. Privacy is waste. One understands, of course . . . not only fear of certain facts being revealed, but fear also of misinterpretation, or one's own carefully formulated interpretation not being shared. But private life, I'm convinced, as it now is, is an anachronism, productive of the general schizophrenia of working together (as the majority do) and living apart; whence periodic association becomes hysterical and valueless, reactive privacy morbidly mystical.

What was most cheering is that there was almost no public manner in the way in which the people spoke. With the reservation that nearly all of them are naturally Welsh-speaking, which accounts for certain peculiarities in expression here and there, the way they spoke in the broadcast is their ordinary way of speaking.

Mr. Styles (who is of course English) said of Croesor:

'. . . everybody knows each other—in this community at least we like each other and help each other on every possible occasion. That's perhaps rather a common characteristic, but the other one, I think, is purely Welsh, and that is that Welsh people are not interested in class distinction or in money-making, though people who go to the seaside resorts on the north coast may sometimes think otherwise. The real Welshman . . . has an artistic side, the shopkeeper who is a chaired bard, and the farmer of the valley here, for instance, who is a first-rate mathematician and poet; that sort of thing that happens in Wales and doesn't happen in England is a sign, I think, of a proper civilization.'

'I love this little valley up here,' said Nellie Jones, 'and I like to entertain the visitors. . . . I sell some minerals and some crisps, and I'm going to make some tea this year.'

P.O'C.: There was a bull last year, wasn't there? He's gone.

N.J.: There was, oh yes, everybody was afraid of him.

O'C.: Why did they let him walk through the village like that, without anything on, you know?

N.J.: He came down from Moelwyn, you know, and then he died at the bottom of the hill. Aye, he rolled down there from the top.

Mrs. Jones of the post office spoke thus: 'I don't go outside the door. Once I close, I close. I sit and read thrillers . . . Oh yes, I like them. I don't like all the love stories, you know. You want something with a bit of foundation.'

O'C.: Ah, but what's the foundation in a thriller?

MRS. J.: Well, you know, there's a bit of excitement . . . the killing and all the rest of it.

O'C.: But, Mrs. Jones, why d'you like the killing?

MRS. J.: Well, I don't know—once you start reading a book you feel
   you want to get to the end of it—well I do.

O'C.: Yes, but the killing—why d'you like that?

MRS. J.: Oh, I don't like it.

O'C.: You don't like it?

MRS. J.: Oh, I don't like it.

O'C.: D'you like not liking it?

MRS. J.: No, I want to have it all after I start reading it.

And she said: 'I think it's better to stay in your own place, isn't it?
Not to go from one house to the other too much because . . . Well,
you see, if you go too often they get tired of you, don't they? . . . And
when you stay in your own place, well you won't do any harm to
anyone, do you? That's what I believe, anyhow—I may be wrong.'
(O'C.: 'It sounds all right.') (And O'C.: 'I expect some even post their
letters elsewhere, don't they?'—'Oh yes, they do. Even parcels, they
walk down the road. . . . There you are—anybody's free and at liberty
to do what they like.') Mrs. Jones hinted at the liberties of such liberty.
   Emrys Williams, farmer with a voice in which nostalgia for times
past sounded like cellos, said: 'It's not as it used to be up here now.'
With alert enterprise, catching at once the drift of his meaning, I
said: 'It's changed a lot?' And he clinched the theme with: 'Quite a lot.'
The village, said Mr. Williams '. . . gets smaller and smaller'. It would
become a holiday place, 'and the community will be finished by
then, and it's the same everywhere, I'm afraid. There was quite a
good community here. . . . There's nearly none at all now. And we're
very disturbed about that. We feel strongly. . . . I'd like the Welsh
language to stay, if it can. And if more English people are coming
here, well then there's no hope of the Welsh language, it will die out,
yes. And then there won't be any mention of the poor old Welsh—
the language will die out. . . . You lose quite a lot when you lose the
language you know. There won't be any literature at all, and that
literature has been of great value and has been all the time. I'm very
keen on poetry although I can't make poetry myself.' And he said:
'Yes, I like him [Dylan Thomas] very much.' Of the Bomb he said
he and the Welsh Nationalist Party were 'up in arms against that.

We're all working for that of course.' And on my suggestion that there was little class feeling and no one to show off to he said: 'No, there isn't, and there's nobody well off with money up here, you know.'

'You don't want to marry?' I asked Auntie Gwen. 'I never thought of it,' she replied. . . . 'Once I'd married I'd have liked children and . . . if someone had come along I suppose I would have.' I mentally saw someone coming along, and turning into the garden gate, and knocking and proposing. Auntie Gwen speaks like someone going for a walk on a summer's day. In the past 'there was more life. We had little meetings in school—they were more lively because there were more competing, and more to do things, you know.' Though Auntie Gwen has been here thirty years she always speaks in English, being English. But I believe she understands Welsh.

The centre of the village, I thought, was Mrs. Margaret Williams, then of the shop, who said she would 'hear all the tales of woe and all the bits and pieces of gossip'. But care was needed in the selection of which pieces to retail, because 'otherwise it could put the place on fire very often. It only wants a match sometimes.' And she had, she said, plenty of matches, but did not strike them. But: 'We're a very small community and we like to live together in peace if we can . . . we're a very happy community now.' Of the Welsh leaving and the English coming (few, actually): 'It's really our own fault that they are leaving. As Welsh people we're not trying to do anything about it. We're just moving into the council houses and the English people are moving into the cottages and into the farmsteads . . . the young men have to drift away and find other work, and the families naturally drift away with them. . . . You never know, it might be a good source of uranium or something like that.' Uranium was found in a seam on the other side of Moelwyn, but was uneconomic to exploit. But Mrs. Williams was very fond of the English, being 'a real Welsh Nationalist, not a person who pretends to be a Welsh Nationalist, who betrays his own country and his own countrymen at the same time, and there are some of those in the Welsh Nationalist Party'. Of the Sunday opening of public houses she said: 'I don't think we ought to have them open on a Sunday, there are six other days for that sort of thing, and—I'm

not against it, I'm not a teetotaller even, but I think Sunday should be
a day of rest and a day of devotion, and for people to think, not only
on Sundays, certainly they must think every other day, but . . .

'Oh no, we're not bored, there's always time to read. I always
think about this place as far from the maddening crowds and ignoble
strife, and of course not everyone can live up in the hills. . . . They
prefer to herd together in these towns and in the council houses, as
I've told you before, which I don't agree with at all. But these little
cottages and little homesteads have much more character than the
postage stamps you see in some of those council estates.' But she also
said: '. . . If anything was brought here—some sort of industry—or
anything was discovered it would give us a much fuller life. Life can be
very empty if there are only a few people. I'm not against the towns
. . . the bigger the community the bigger the scope for doing welfare
work . . . because it's very selfish to shut yourself up in a little—well,
it's the same as the monks do in the monasteries even. I can't understand
that they can do any good at all by shutting themselves there; they say
they can do more good by praying and that sort of thing than by
living amongst the rank and file.'

'That's a beautiful voice,' said the engineer at Bangor when he
heard the faraway—'Celtic', he said—lilt of Edith's voice. Like a bird
in winter on a wire she sang:

'I came here from the crowd of London in order to write a book.
I want to write a book in which I record faithfully and truly as
possible all the things that I've known, and I've known a lot. I've
known a lot and I've seen a lot and I thought this is the place to do it,
but since I came all I do is clean out grates, clean out birds' nests from
chimneys, sweep floors, repair old walls. But when I look out on those
hills at the back of the valley, I think these things and the stars at night,
these things are fundamental and absolute and in the days of synthetic
pleasure, in the days of celluloid amusement, in the days of false violence,
trumped-up drama, I think it's possible to get back to one's self. I don't
know what I mean by "self".' And: '. . . Small trivialities loom up
extremely important when you're alone and when you're with a few
people; trivialities which you would absolutely not notice normally,
in your ordinary surroundings in a city; little moods of people, tones

of voices, expressions in eyes, become extraordinarily important, almost as important as one's own ghosts, and ghosts haunt one at night: ghosts of oneself.' (I: 'Yes, I dare say you've got a good population there, Edith, a good ghostly population. Do they come tramping through the night?') Edith: 'They do.' ('And do they make a lot of noise? And what do they accuse you of, Edith?') Edith: 'They accuse me of wasting my time in talks, idleness, but they accuse me of something more; they accuse me of a very ancient guilt.' ('Yes, and what is that?') Edith: 'That I won't disclose.' But, she agreed, it 'gives me a place on the human map'.

Talking to Edith before the microphone gave me another of those switches from 'private' into 'public' that can make such an interesting experience: the 'public' and 'private' prove delightfully mysterious (and tribal in their fond differences). An element of recitation adheres to 'public', and one of almost cloacal conspiracy to 'private'. I'd been very private with Edith, ten years ago in Suffolk and continuously since. We found the 'public' situation slightly chilling; but I was surprised at the enduring substance of her manner and her statements; the difference between the two was oddly slight. Her voice was a little more precise and more Irish in its lilt; that was how she used the recitational exigencies. But I felt possessed of an inquisitorial asperity, as though I had her at my mercy; how much rancour I must have built up against her. Why? Because she had done a great deal for me, and I no doubt feared her presentation of the bill. Her influence had been considerable and, like one ten years younger, I wanted to be 'independent'; a chronic kind of dependence, indeed. After this, we found much of the old communion restored. Of all people I have known, Edith Young most expertly can assess the economics of human relationships.

'Public and private' continued to find their modified relationship for me during the recording of 'Croesor'. All in all, I found them far less distinct than I had 'cynically' supposed; I found people far more forthcoming than I had expected. My own wild urge to communicate had made me forget the general possession of this saving grace of individualism. Like waters, people love to find their common level through expressing their differences to one another.

Moreover, David proved to be a subtle seducer of initially locked egos; gentle, naive and charmingly eccentric in manner, with the absent-mindedness that tells people the heart must be good for the brain so to leave it alone, not a soul could suspect him of anything wicked. The result sounded like overheard gossip; but I gather not all were pleased with such informality.

Being different is so exciting that finding we are alike is the only possible and bearable discovery. So the foam returns into the beer.

Benevolent, episcopal a little, very eighteenth-century in his enjoyment of nourishing periods, Clough Williams-Ellis explained something of his stewardship of the amenities; their preservation is mostly due to himself, upon which I have written at greater length in another chapter. Said he: 'I do regard the Croesor Valley as my ancestral valley and I certainly regard myself as part of its indigenous fauna.' He certainly looked like that; out of wooded rocks his sudden appearance would be subconsciously unsurprising. A touch of the (white) warlock about him; long and easily active in build, his eyes rather closed to many degrees of human intimacy (he prefers buildings and landscapes, as objects of interest, to people), his heart, and he himself (within) appear well secreted; their incalculable romanticism appears only in nuances of emphasis and bursts of utterance from their masonic protection. But the not only great but complex depths of this romanticism are all evident in the gardens of Plâs Brondanw, which remind me forcibly of the sets in Jean Cocteau's early film, *La Belle et la Bête*. Vivid ghosts inhabit hedges and urns, statues and ponds and fountains, and give them an edge not as finite as their apparently dead state would normally have. As in La Bête's grounds around his palace, a wounded hero of life has his living ghost in things called dead; and the peace therein is inhabited thus. So the 'ramparts' of Plâs Brondanw suggest those of a castle holding out against bad times, and within the ramparts the secret life of the preserved goes nimbly, gaily, subtly, on. Like his house is Williams-Ellis, an example in the conservation of energy for its blithely profitable canalizations, the ones he has un-remittingly cherished in as authentic a fight against ugliness as anyone we are likely to know. For the matter is far beyond what we rather belittlingly (or inflatedly) call 'aesthetic'. At the basis of his concern is the certainty and the knowledge that ugly places make ugly people; something the world at large is slowly coming to recognize, after an interval of several hundreds of years. But this all-absorbing concern has made him a little out of human, in the sense of familiar; because, as I have said, the place and architecture are more interesting, probably more alive, than are most people to him.

'It's awfully difficult,' he said (of escapers from cities), 'because the minority realize the uncivilized squalor of our great cities for instance, and wants to escape; and where is there for them to escape to except into what we consider our countryside? And, of course, they don't understand country manners—they bring urbanism with them and unless they're controlled and—still better—taught appreciation, they really destroy, by their clumsiness, what they love or would love if they only understood it. . . . And it's a unique little community, and one doesn't want it—I think—to grow any larger than is viable.' I suggested mass incursions would ruin the place; said he: 'I'd say—not more free access up the drive.' He owns the drive; to which Mr. John Jones was edited to interject: 'One of the special difficulties of farming in Croesor is the question of access by road. In our farm one of the access roads is through Croesor and in order for anything to be brought to the farm—a cattle lorry or a load of hay or fertilizer— it's necessary to pass under the archway—the lodge, near Plâs Brondanw—and it's impossible for such loads to pass through, so that our farming is always done at this—with this disability . . .' But a few months later the arch was bypassed.

We used a tape and a half on Mr. Bob Owen, but unfortunately I haven't the transcript with me. His voice lit up the air like no one else's.

The participants liked the results, which was what mattered most to me. After it I felt a little more at home; always a foreigner, of course, but tolerable, perhaps. But my daughter is a native and will most probably speak Welsh. Never enthusiastic about schools, I noted that the little one at Croesor is an exception to the kind I know and dislike. My horror has always been that extraction from a subject to be learned called 'discipline' which, being extracted, is then applied as a technique of coercion; it being assumed that no subject could ever be interesting

enough to children without this coercion. I felt convinced that Mrs.
Morgan, the teacher, had proved otherwise. In fact when recording I
laboured the point too much.

o'c.: Do you punish them at all, Mrs. Morgan? How do you punish
   them, I mean?
MRS. M.: Well, I never get the occasion to punish them.
o'c.: You don't really?
MRS. M.: No, not really. They're very, very good children.
o'c.: No thrashing?
MRS. M.: No thrashing, no.
o'c.: You don't stand them in the corner?
MRS. M.: No, never.
o'c.: You don't give them extra lessons—nothing?
MRS. M.: Never.
o'c.: They like—they actually like——
MRS. M.: They like school.
o'c.: Good heavens!

And little Kathleen Williams was a visitor (aged eleven): 'I like
English talking best 'cos you can learn it better . . . I knew somebody
. . . they came here and they was here about five weeks and they learnt
it [Welsh]. Yes, they learned Welsh straight away and they stayed
here 'cos they knew it.' She went to Mrs. Morgan's school. The
children are bilingual.

The atmosphere, compared with schools in London I've seen, is
extraordinary: spotlessly clean, quiet without being inhibiting, and
the children a quite wonderful combination of independence and
courtesy; resembling, I thought, Neill's children at Summerhill.

The children carried on something to be discerned in Mrs. Jones of
the post office, who had said that when she closed, she closed. What
she closed against was clear enough—a world that she thought had
changed for the worse, even in Croesor. A small, rather dumpy
woman, modest, even humble, and proud as fire also, she seems to
commune more with memories than with present life. An older kind,
'inner-directed' still, she has a quiet pessimism about the world around

an inner optimism about her own (spiritual) adventure in it. Her old world is gone for ever; she has much poetry in her soft but brisk tones, much sweetness in her eyes. A very soft clear voice, as of one putting babies to bed; putting to bed, I imagined, certain young hopes of her own; she polishes her brasses. She has an innocence and a naivety very rare today, and is probably as good as a child. All this, though consciously remote from the children in school, is nevertheless absolutely clear in their singing voices, which we recorded. There again Mrs. Jones's hopes come brightly out of trumpets to the sky: hopes that are organic, constitutional and quite pre-mental. They sang like the morning; few voices in the world can be as lovely as those of Welsh children. They have the essence of courage and of hope—life's song never changing in the beginning, down the years lurching to gravel undertones, ruptured into embarrassed syncopation, nervously exhilarated into impossibly shrill heroism of principles but not of the whole man, and saddled down with sumptuous tragedy in reaction; the immense unreality of emotion, once the primal and organic reality is gone.

To revert to the distinctions between 'public' and 'private' manners, my own experience until I came to live in Croesor had been aggressively private. Sometimes in my disturbed adolescence I had had 'attacks' of living publicly—through the total absence of intimate associates or relatives. The behaviours this involved seemed very near to madness, which even a small root to personal privacy turned at once into humour. The good soldier Schweik thus plays at being public, a marionette faithfully exhibiting all officially enjoined reflexes. So, if we were to compose out of the public behaviour and utterances of our own public figures a 'real' man, allowing nothing for his private life, we should have Schweik without the humour. Hitler was of this type; the painter Nolde seems to have painted him in anticipation. Conversely the completely private man is the nihilist so well known to literature, and whom the Beats now emulate. There is yet a pretension, and/or a general conspiracy in agreeing that the public man is entirely there in his public behaviour and utterances, his publicized moral code; though we know the opposite. Yet he speaks as a whole man. But we know that he presents a cleaned surface. This most unpropitious cleavage between the public and the private man comes of many influences. Primary among them is the excessive weight of tradition, through which every growing child is handed down successive stereotypes of public actuality, against which his private self becomes increasingly conspiratorial. The private life is, despite those great advertisements of democracy which credit a man with the power of ruling himself, unrelated to the public one. Only a community identifying private with public interest can resolve this sterile dichotomy. Among other factors, it is a predominant cause of crime; the private man is anarchist, the public man is totalitarian. So the private man uses the mask of the public man for his private ends. Many certified schizophrenics must have been people unable to weld these incompatible selves into a working whole; hence, for instance, 'delusions of grandeur', a straightforward, ingenuous self-identification with a conceptually public man of the unorientated private one. The private man must tend to identify himself with God, and the public man with Caesar.

But Croesor is a simple community. In a village of this size, especially a Welsh village, public and private behaviour tend very much to be identical—because, it seems, everything sooner or later becomes known of the private self to the public. But Croesor is exceptional. That weather-eye ever open for sin (the spotting of which brings such moral dividends—the haul counted in the virtuous house) is here much laxer than (a traveller's glance would estimate) it is in any nearby town or village. Its decline is much responsible for this laxity, which brings us to the old-fashioned, more positive aspect of the private-public dichotomy: that in public people honestly portrayed their conceivedly best selves: a proclamation of their ideal. All the best was once for 'public'; now, all the smoothest. The best has retreated again to within doors for the very few still interested, and there become something quite esoteric. In Croesor a sliver of this old function of the 'public' is evident; and a better balance is maintained between that and private behaviour. There is a small hard core of older Croesor residents that still maintains a semblance of service to Victorian morality and a rigidly maintained public segregation from private reality—a handful, perhaps two families. They probably 'face

God' with fervour, meet their critic and take his advice (which well enough is in accord with survival exigencies). They carve, still, fine lines upon their passions, singing maybe sometimes with aspiration. Hypocrisy is a poor word for this life; decadence is a better one for what follows when people become 'emancipated'—into nowhere and nothing. Small as it is, it is the modern and 'progressive' element in Croesor that suggests what little there is of the tawdry and the meretricious—a phenomenon quite beyond the narrow and, by now, stereotyped logistics of progressive beliefs. For man *cannot* function well without aspiration; when the divine goes, the sub-human takes its place until something else is found—the new, co-operative community. England now suffers horribly thus. Everyone is becoming 'advanced', seeing through in order to see nothing in their fellow men, seeing through to the gargoyle reflection of their officially supported egotism. The fashion, for long in England, in Europe, in the Western world, has been disillusionment, which is the parent of nihilism, and not profound.

In Mrs. Morgan, however, we find a synthesis all too rare; something progressive, yet with the advantages of a moral code. Her children exercise a wide spontaneity which is not confused with licence; expressive of this civilized atmosphere, for instance, was the solo Margaret Williams' little boy sang for us. To be heard, definite, stated, something of the dream of this (and any) people: an implicit belief in something for which we have the inadequate word 'purity'—involving a fine discarding of the equivocal, an identification of energy with honour as the essence of humanness, a reaching-out to new worlds and new knowledge. That the preservation of this integrity seems to demand some measure of frustration (in sexual matters) may be conceded. Yet what happens when we have 'freedom' (by which is usually meant specifically sexual freedom) *without* a society that can exploit it, that can properly employ the energies liberated by such freedom? We have decadence; for as a private discipline, unsupported by social forms, freedom is too much for us: only freedom shared is 'viable'. Individually, it is licence, an anomaly. The capitals of Europe are littered with freedom fans, people allegedly uninhibited; and what happens? Their freedom becomes their greatest inhibition against *any* social orientation whatsoever. Not because freedom is 'wrong'; but because it demands a form of society very much in advance of our own to contain it creatively. So, we must remember, England's gathering emancipation—especially in sexual life—is, as the bishops say, a sign of its decline—from what it was. The waters are bursting through the worn-out dams. Dams are bad; floods are worse. The taste for life comes as whisky, goes as waste down the drains. We have reached the end of a civilization of repressive ethics and the mutual exploitation that goes with such ethics; but we have arrived at nothing better. Croesor has so far missed the emancipation. With luck it may leap across the mess of 'emancipation' into the new world: with luck. To help it, it has the Welsh health, due to the fact that the Welsh have missed some of the advantages of the Industrial Revolution, especially in the North. As competitors, they are children; they are still stained with old-fashioned community values. What would carry them over would be their 'old-fashioned' drive to asceticism which, as we know, is retrograde. But life deals in functions, not in absolutes. What's good for the goose may be bad for the gander. Over a flood, perhaps only the spirit, that *creative* aberration of humanity, could carry them. All who understand the essence of progress must appreciate the beauties decocted, at so immense a price, out of its apparent opposite, Puritanism. As suggested earlier, it is precisely the rituals of Puritanism that, in Welsh song, are powerful enough to re-connect with the pagan vitality and imagination of the Welsh: as though they had fashioned a boat for their pristine selves to cross the waters. Since a whole world has invested in this tortuous experiment of spirit at the expense of body, it would be reasonable to see some present functions of it. The answer, certainly, isn't that preposterous individualistic collapse into freedom that is making London, for instance, so hideous: a freedom only the other side of a financially motivated Puritanism that preceded it.

In the voice of the Williams child was the quality we call heaven; an 'illusion', we say: not so, but an imagination. The intellectual concept may be an illusion; but the force and the feeling are not. They are realistic in the proper sense, in that reality is what we make—tomorrow out of yesterday. Its sureness expresses in its unstrivingness it *arrives*, it does not so much seek: it will make the world in its own image, purely for the needs of equilibrium and something more . . . the something more that creates the need for new equilibrium. It is unstriving as was Lawrence's best writing, making him one of the most *convincing* of all writers, and not by the force of argument, but by a style suggesting willing, gay inevitability: *amor fati* precedes control of fate; fatalism is its abortion. Religion, to repeat, is the heart of a heartless world; that world had better gain its head before it dispenses with that heart. They are not inimical; the new, forming head is but a development from that heart, its social application. Only Puritans make debauchees; only socialism makes men. Till then, maybe Puritans had better stay such. Their development lies in socialism, not in this world, which has only tawdry 'emancipation' to offer them.

Thus exceptionally in Croesor may one begin to see that success, in our conventional sense, is not necessarily inimical to inner truth.

Whereas the town at dead of night will uncoil the day's personalia and leave a shivering bobbin of humanity without strength or meaning, the country stumps the undressed self at the same time into the more poignant hole of mortality, of a man at a certain stage in a journey, going to death: which the town obscures. High on the quarry road the black shadow of the sharp mountain induces one to think of some basic facts of life, highly significant among which is death, the slate-wiper. There, in the dark, the cold and the wind, one may lose the personalia, the elaborate character, the passion for goodness and its contemporary exegesis, the reasons for wickedness, and wonder on them. Life seems there such a busy matter; so inbound, so deluded into sensations of immortality. One looks down on it, lit up on one's busy expression, so horribly lacking in perspective; one wonders at the years-long muddle, at the busy protest, the apathetic conformity; their contrast begins to dull. How and why is so much made of so short a journey, with so absolute a finale? Continuity of generations, of course, is the answer; and yet this business of being a link in a chain does too much to favour that image at the expense of the other truth: that we are ones who will never recur; that is the other truth so effective in rendering down the operas of morality and ambition in a second of perception, to the point of nihilism. It is but a half-truth; the mind that conceives it is itself a social product; yet at the service of as much an individual as we are forced—always forced—to be. That chain will be stronger by one link taking a view that owes least to knowable tradition, and thereby fitting in with the greater and unknown one. Culture may be a collection of medals, a hat at the mercy of newer cultural winds, a stormproof coat of self-esteem; or the node of perception. Because we are of some rudimentary form of society, some incipient community mostly unborn, we may stand and perceive alone; and that solitude arises from community is in no way inimical to it; perspectives of that individuality are for the community.

Solitude brings an ideal of itself; of non-participation. But that's a misinterpretation of the truer ideal envisioned in solitude. The true ideal is one of authentic response, one that plays no game other than the truth's. Part of the truth is compassion; and there's the rub. Adolescents and cynics will sharpen the polemical destructive weapon; and there's plenty of alien dough to receive it. But does the 'spirit of truth' express itself polemically? I don't know. From the core of polemic for a good cause we may strip polemic for individual self-aggrandizement—if we strip hard: often the cause comes away with the individualism. But does the good cause come to fruition through polemic and struggle? Perhaps; yet I think the days of this kind of struggle are numbered. Annihilation is too easy to permit of an easy use. As individuals, in degree of our being so, we have warred all our lives; to live is to war, or to collude for an uneasy slumber with the enemy, which is then internal war. And yet, what subtleties of perception and thought haven't we lost thereby? The saints perfected a technique of inspiration from God. Truth, into which God has proliferated, seems no longer single, but borne on the backs of innumerable disciplines; as though man, through a superfluity of crutches, had lost the imagination to think he could walk entire. But the proliferation of disciplines, which is in their immaturity (though they render suspect certain anachronistic simplifiers, those who still pretend to inhale a single truth), nevertheless have an atavistic interest in their segregation. They inflame their hides for the exaltation of preciously independent significance. Those who see singleness of truth

Croesor

are usually the mad or the charlatans; those may sometimes be the guardians of a forgotten unity. For lack of a goal makes each player his captain.

As soon as a thought is born, in a difficulty discouraging to further births, it must be argued against all other thoughts in its field, forfeiting that important period of maturation whereby it might become so much more. As babes in armour are thoughts; thus too they perpetuate a struggle that maturity would have convened into a harmony.

Much of contemporaneity is inescapable, including its bastard misconception of individuality as endemically warring. And yet, I think we should delay an ultimate acceptance unto death. The best war is against this time, to co-operate with longer periods.

Polemic beyond its proper uses becomes a conspiracy to war.

The Welsh mountains bring a sagacious, positive sort of solitude, far too good for melancholy; such emotions waste such an experience. Solitude brings the messages: that of belonging, and that of not belonging, because one is individually going to death. Belonging, because everything one is comes from others; not belonging, because everything one does with what one is, is made alone. Actions, which must include thoughts, are done individually, out of a common inheritance, to which they return. Gloom is subjective; the Welsh mountains are not gloomy, can manage well enough without any of our little anthropomorphisms. They are wild, ravaged, untidy. When the elements whip up, they are wilder still; to the wind and the rain, they oppose an iron permanence. Their message again, in storm, is sweet and peaceful, like any recurrence. The rages of Nature are innocent and clean, spotlessly whistling their queer tunes. They have much to impart—permanence, and transitoriness. Permanence in the mind, I think; but not in one mind.

Croesor is cradled in the mountains and the people, as people will, enclose themselves away. Their homes are nest-like, their minds will dwell not on large things but, protectively, on small; they join in the huddle of humanity. And yet their central eyes know these mountains, and thus are clear and impersonal. Our first view of the aerial spectrality of this well-washed and winded place, so bleakly and so beautifully set, was not mistaken.

G

8

Bryn Hyfryd

AT TY CAPEL we were visiting, but we came to Bryn to live, which involved the easy dislocation of all the sensationally novel aspects of Croesor. That in turn meant that the limited area of Bryn Hyfryd would slowly connect through present into past areas of our inhabitation; Croesor would inevitably join the world from here. Time would with space come leaking in through the walls—it sounds like, and must be related to, hissing in the ears. Then our eyes would no longer be stopped by the spectacularly new; they would focus again behind 'surfaces', allowing 'surfaces' to amalgamate with past ones, be comparable with them. And eventually, perhaps, when our focus was too far behind these appearances, we would have to move on to nourish our eyes.

If you imagine us standing still and facing our front windows, our walls about us, you would see from left to right Edith Young (who indulges in the arts), myself and family, Nellie Jones and family (five children). We would all be staring at you as you walked along the lane.

Edith was not very evident at Ty Capel, was so at Bryn, though she stays only for the summer and odd holidays. Having known her for ten years, she tends to drag Croesor backward through that time for me, or did. But that is now over. After initial hostility on my part we made a truce and agreed to listen to each other.

Bryn Hyfryd, I should explain, is about a quarter of a mile outside the village, nearer Cnicht and Moelwyn. It is a block of four cottages, the last of which is a burned-out shell. Across the river and a little way up the hill is Ben and David Williams' farm, Croesor Bach. There's another farm further into the valley, belonging to Mr. Cledwyn Roberts, who, I believe, does not like the English. This might be most perceptive, but he regards me as English; perhaps that is also perceptive.

The village's only two drinkers are the Williams brothers, who rejoice once a week in an orderly manner. The men in Croesor, otherwise, do not drink. I don't know why—not for health reasons, I don't think. Probably in an association of virtue with abstemiousness— with which I can sympathize. But this puts the breweries in an awkward moral predicament. But I don't think that the men of Croesor have done anything to save the brewery men—like most Christians, their own salvation comes first. It should occur to Christians that this is unchristian. (Parenthetically, let it be remarked that Stavrogin, who disdained salvation, is reasonably Christian.) Morality is actually something no one except Moral Rearmers are practical about; and they are immoral.

As residents the simplicity of the people of Croesor wore off in our eyes, though whenever I went to London and returned thence I saw it again. Their delight for me lay in their ardent particularization.

We found that there are many people living alone, or widows with children, in Croesor; that, so far, there exists no couple in a suburbanly interesting condition of conflict. Hence, a lack of drama prevails. Even sexual adventures appear to be either few or non-existent. In the year we have been in Bryn we have noticed the wells of gossip drying up. Nothing happens. Or news may be, for instance, that someone's dog has killed two sheep and none is saying whose dog it is, though everyone knows. A. S. Neill (whose school was evacuated to near here during the war) told me he thought the Welsh quite remarkable humbugs. They would, he said, pack the golf clubs in the boot to avoid the reputation of sinning on Sunday. No doubt true in a sense (though showing off to God—or neighbours?—is understandable)— but less so of Croesor. Are they at all humbugs? I've suggested their sung *vertu* is real; so it is—and that it connects their chapel rituals with their pagan vitals; which is true. May it be from this that their attitude to the appearances and performances of virtue are curiously accountant? I think they are so; I sense a very fine calculation as to what degree of virtue shall be shown to whom. Under the virtue is the dark, rather grinning look in the eye; under chapel virtue, often, there's a most primitive look. The Welsh are ambipsychic.

Bryn goes to chapel sometimes, Croesor Bach rarely. Nellie occasionally goes; Mr. Styles has been seen (out of the corner of the eye that rightly was looking away) gardening on Sunday. We have done the washing on the day. We have even done the writing. If so fine a point can be made, I think the Bryn Hyfryd area is, all in all, less moral than the village proper; perhaps because of its remoteness from the chapel. This would not include Mr. Cledwyn Roberts and his family, however—not at all. It is not, of course, that we are immoral, in Bryn Hyfryd: it could not be that. Is it that perhaps we are wiser? That on no account could we possibly imagine God being impressed by ritual? Or could He be? Well, since He was convened to be, perhaps He is. I am not religious, now not in any sense; to me, religion is intellectual slumming. It is the flight from perception to belief; and belief belongs to feet, not to the intelligence. All my life I have regarded church-going as mass insanity. I can see its function, some of its function. But the world would be better with a real community, and without the exercises of faith in a divine one.

Among the most disastrous effects of religion, evident I believe in the Welsh, is the intellectual schism created by a division of divine and earthly reality. It means that the proper source of genius is barred, incarcerated in the concept of divinity; it makes the earthly reality rather sterile, mechanistically materialistic. So, further, it places too great a faith in the factual part of culture—I think Welsh intellectuals tend to be far too scholastic. For creation belongs either to God or man. Belief in God inhibits the digestion of factual education into understanding, and further dissociates understanding from social action.

In Croesor, for instance, intelligence is associated with memory; the native true thing (evident to me in, for instance, our Raymond) is ignored when it won't serve as a fly-paper to facts. Education being too associated with status, national genius is wasted in the attempt to be formally educated. More than in England, formal education is confused with creative talent. Education is a tool only; it dresses up as the soul of man.

Bryn Hyfryd is nearly as far away from these rigidities as Croesor is from the world I know. You could call it a near-slum area, I suppose, if three rather dilapidated cottages can constitute a slum, when the fresh air blows most of the decomposition away. But Bryn Hyfryd is amazingly unrespectable. Mountains seem nearer than men. So they are, in a purely social sense.

We have very much to do with our neighbour, Nellie Jones,[1] whom all would agree is a very simple woman; she herself, however, has explained to my wife that she is deep. Anyway she is simple enough to have missed the refinements of certain atrophied senses, whose worn ashes constitute some nuances of civilization. Nellie is aware of living in a spider's web of Rules, which the remote They have concocted— why, she couldn't say, which is something we have in common.

Nellie looks and lives rather like a gypsy, though I don't think she is at all of that race. She lives in great and zestful confusion with five children, but is herself capable of remarkable serenity in the goings-on bound to occur with so many young ones. When she speaks to me I note a constantly tentative amusement at what she says and at what I reply; she suggests it could all be amusing, but it might be as well not to laugh until, perhaps, They had sent us one of their licences to be amused. I admire the discretion of this, obviously the only way to get round Them—a Schweikian tactic. It gives her a little girl's slightly artfully contrived ignorance before grown-ups, an air that, we know, is sometimes useful, grown-ups being so susceptible to their own admiration, even if presumed into by others. Gazing respectfully, therefore, Nellie is at her most amused and amusing, but would drop this at the first warning from Them. She is good at helping people on with their egos when they've come in from the cold—a service of course whose recognition is inimical to its success; but Nellie is aware of much self-protection to be gained by such helping on with. I am also aware of this.

She is also gifted with the ability (which I am acquiring too) of talking at great length from the support of the door frame, the garden wall, or the weather. Her talk is gently nuzzling, as though to say: love

[1] In North Wales 'gypsy' has an unfortuntate connotation due to the prevalence of the 'diddyki' [sic]—half-gypsy. I mean, in regard to Mrs. Jones, that she resembles the rare Romany in features.

is somewhere but I don't quite know where; perhaps I have mislaid it in the kitchen? The failure to find whatever she seeks naturally helps her to seek for ever, which is to talk at length. She talks as flowers are flung in festivals in happier lands where there's enough organic joy to occasion such flinging. She will talk like this and will condole with misfortune and exclaim upon tragedies in the same birdlike chirrups of sedate rapture, bobbing on her wire for all to hear. We compare shovelfuls of dingy disaster from the *Express* with her loads from the *Herald*; we did fine the other day with extraordinary goings-on in which curates and parsons and curates' wives seemed to have been rolling over each other in a Babylonian vestry. 'It goes to show,' said Nellie. 'They're as bad as we are.' Worse.

Nellie's five children are brought up on the most modern, libertarian principles. They do more or less what they like, to such an extent that they appear sometimes not to like it. Most times, however, they do, and when not passionately screaming are a happy crew, extremely individuated. Given a frustration, however, they tend to jump at it. Raymond, whom I emphatically call wicked to protect myself from his angelic voice and face, shines with honour when told he may not have something—that is, he shines later. Give him whatever he wants and he may saunter off with substantiated misanthropy. It's possible they don't sleep enough, eat too many sweets; and yet they emanate a kind of security rare to see, and a capacity of absorbed interest as rare.

They move all in a piece, not with airs of observation trailing behind; they are compact and swift. They are, on the whole, a good example of what the absence of the repressive discipline does—when they meet it in school they quickly learn to adopt the manners of obedience without the beliefs associated with it: I mean in their 'big' school, after Mrs. Morgan's. It is simple to idealize; and yet, once again, one sees growing up as growing down in children. Raymond especially suggests possibilities not likely to mature, through circumstances. But all children are especially lucky here. They have the school, which they all appear to like; comparative immunity from the more abstruse shorthands in violence; safety of mountains. They have also Mrs. Williams, ex-shop, as an established centre of congregation.

It is perhaps a little socially dangerous to be exposed to less than the normal amount of depravity at a tender age; because one's unemployed 'folly' is very unprotected.

A pantechnicon of the old order of drama is my other neighbour (in summer), Edith. Her face is the scarred battlement of the old individual against the modern mass. A relic of the gone middle-class illusion of self-responsibility and that immense personal significance that reached its apotheosis in D. H. Lawrence's philosophy—the self that swallowed, in one last Gargantuan attempt, worlds (to find more worlds frisking outside the dining-room)—Edith now suffers the passing trains of standard lives, as she deems them. With a curiously baleful glance (hard to detect), she even boards one now and then, quite grinning with contemporary vacuity, ease of progress. Her heart is of course elsewhere; possibly, it always was, since childhood. No mature situation has been quite to its liking; it looked in always through the windows at the scenes in which her grown-up self participated, and eventually brought her outside again. She has had a short bout of 'hardening', but I suspect this is a last rally, and that she will relax again; no one has so substantial and unchangeable a nature as she. As ten years ago, we sailed down to the pub at Llanfrothen to pick up the threads, myself a little more careerist, a little more complacent; she, not much different. It was never ideas that we had in common, but a certain endemic exile from, I should imagine, practically everything that goes on; obversed, as is usual with such people, by an intense curiosity about every detail of everyone's lives. Our exile can have little to do with our very different upbringing and circumstances— though we both suffered from off-putting elders. I can remember my guardian complaining testily that I was not 'there', where he was. True enough.

Edith also, I think, was not 'there'. But 'there' is pretty awful premises, at least from the outside view—a view never earned, but, as suggested, endemic. Edith's soul has the least fatness of souls I have tasted; it is very un-English, in its lack of avoirdupois. (Consider, for instance, the English literary critical soul, spread on its huge hams, its oily big eyes unctuous with counter-creative lusts; or, even funnier, the souls of the Reverends, who understand a fellow's weaknesses. The best English soul is to be found in the upper Civil Service, I suspect.) Consequently Edith is allergic, like my mother, to the souls of English males, which are serious departments. I've no doubt we started in the same hopeless error of expecting a sort of divine human family, and met these plump souls to explain to us how much better the actual dog-fight was. We also lack the queer grind that goes into careerism, the so-serious contemplation of one's powers, and their dismal marketing. We lack too, perhaps, the wonderful sense of our rights, which makes people sit up on hind legs (like conservative trades-unionists) and demand more sugar.

In Croesor, yet, I sensed a slight staleness in our old discussions. My own congestion was lessened in the last few years; a little strategically, that last year when Edith was down, I felt unable to be as scornful of any kind of success as, equally strategically, I had been in the old days: just *in case* something of mine sold. (But now I have cleared up that problem to my satisfaction, and reached Jean Cocteau's conclusion: success demands the permanent sense of failure. Failure . . . is nearly divine; it attends an endless future.) We both shy at the extraordinarily well-dressed body of current Philistinism, in the haute couture of its 'artistic sensibility'; at the *gross* appreciation of art as, quite definitely, a substitute for beautiful living (living with sense, order and purpose), and as cosmetic to smear Philistine snouts. Who, I ask, can compete with British ham-handedness in their treatment of certain delicacies? In their contemplation of favoured *angsts* in the 'literary' Press? In their wincingly fine categorizations that angels fear to measure? No wonder E. M. Forster closed down.

Then we were both very much of the thirties, and still retain some of its sweetly optimistic pantheism; in preference to the new opportunism, the quite blind mole's belief in this 'prosperity' (already groggy), and the exploitation, again, of 'art' to defraud a materialistic progress with the gloss of the ineffable. How sprayed around today are 'spiritual' values on the carcasses of Caliban—man's last, utmost, humbuggery. Wait till the slump: familiar squeals will return. Whereas the thirties, despised by today's streamlined committee-men of culture and 'progress' (whither?), *believed*—at least—in a new world of co-operation. And we have instead of this? Gaitskell. Yes, the thirties was a good dream, and all good dreams are prophetic and come true. The post-war years will, not long ahead, be seen for the immense ugliness of their intellectual life, their chain-store culture and their horror of the future.

All of which has so much by-passed Edith, who still, possibly against her expressed convictions, retains the sense of the organic unity of beauty and life, still knows the invincible therapy of beauty, and the incomparable beauty of truth's rare moments, which come like the light, and are never forgotten; as Stephen Spender said of integrity: 'living faithfully according to a pattern and a rule which one knows only at moments and then knows one has known always'. That is true. In her way Edith has found herself perhaps really *condemned* to the practice of this truth; for her ardent endeavours to do otherwise have been several, and failures, like mine.

Hence in Croesor she is not a stranger; she has something of the Welsh, who also, here, retain this 'old-fashioned' notion of integrity, this anachronistic and secret passion for an order, non-authoritarian, such as the world has not yet seen but will see; when individual and community are prosperously integrated, when the barbarism of bright aggressive individualism is seen for the incompenent fraud it is.

She remains a delightful person, naive in a welter of wiles, artless in artfulness, and able to be happy at a moment's notice: explode a child's heart and you see the stars, humanly internalized, which die in the civic chest. Rimbaud was such an explosion.

Where, I could say with Edith, is gone the simplicity of profound applications in art? And we may contemplate the branded 'personalities' and their tritely spewed 'problems': basic, the problem of 'being an individual' (a cuttlefish?) when one's neighbour is similarly employed; the fraudulent problem, in which 'individual' is extracted from community for his transcendental patenting. Profundities of his squirms! The wonder of his *difference!* He shows signs of exhaustion. All fools have one thing in common: they feel different.

Ends and beginnings? From none as much as Edith do I get the sense of time; she, like the sea, is a clock, of a special, spatial kind. We think of dawns gingered up by ambition, of ends fatalized by haste. If one lived gradually one would die well; we waste in fake dramas—of imminent war, murder, luscious adulteries—dramas of what the skirt hides, of what it reveals, money and 'love' (which learns to carry its camera with it); the whole package grubbily miscalled life till we are braised into the automatic discharge of fatal responses to these packaged stimuli; while above invisible big brother drones: 'You are individual . . . all different.' How to wrench oneself out of this filthy blackmail into conformist 'thought', decked out in rags of personalism? With the comic operatic nightmare of some alleged 'totalitarianism' that will take our individuality away from us? Surely, a burden willingly to be discharged. For the unwilling, life is a conspiracy, requiring immense strategy, and a cunning that must not fall in love with itself; we have allies, however; some in the 'less developed' (less atrophied, less canned) communities, such as Croesor. A strategy it is, this life of the not so much anti-conformist (they always end up by playing 'the game', once their fee is settled) as the nonconformist. And, as one ages, one sees most blessedly some rewards of one's incapacity to be decent and canned; a liberal jollity in thought, a lack of fear of where one's thoughts may take one; an almost indiscriminate liking for people, because one automatically discounts the proffered personality to meet the sacredly human; a lack, eventually, of direful, exhausting competition. Once one has perfected one's exile from the excrescential conformism, one may totally immerse oneself among people without fear of death in *that* 'life'; whereas the 'straightforward' rebel (the tart waiting for his fee) leads, let us say, a very strange life indeed; rather spectral. The rewards of going one's way are immense; they are that Way, which becomes larger than 'one's'. *That* was the virtue of religion, which progress has not substituted, which co-operation will. For the extraordinary thing about life is that it is not important, but the opposite: it is vital, properly careless, profligate and therefore economical, incautious and therefore wise. How not to save must be the beginning of wisdom; how to give, the end of it. All the great truths are well known; fame is the time-blessed technique of enduring them unscathed. To know has become the technique of not applying; the brow is levered high above the body, and holds nothing but holy nonsense, so that it is in no wise incommodious to think; no action will follow.

So, we pause very long at the brink of such a civilization as only few have imagined, to which the gateway is peace. Edith and I, toddlers with an odd thought, return from the pub; with the poor pilgrims' *élan vital*, which is a moderate amount of beer, inside us, we're drenched, at night up the winding road, by the stars and their proof of ultimate fulfilment; so much beauty, so *concrete*, visible, actual, brilliant and vast. Our breasts are drenched by the far lights, by tolerant, all-wise time, who nurses mankind to the maturities of peace and the work of art. In a place so vast where the brain is properly apparent for what it is: a tentacle of genius touching infinity; and the heart, who houses so competently the love of this adventure, so signally non-recurrent individually, so beatifically recurrent universally. Then, heart and brain, love and thought, reach their moment of identity, which is their proper condition. For to love is to think; thought is love's apotheosis, and there's no ultimate distinction; the brain stretches out from its hutchlike confinement enforced upon it by our competitive neurosis. It walks and runs, it flies and sings, splashes of light tincture it, there's height and no depth for it, but the incredible and long flash of the moment; as Nietzsche, that most unclerical man, so well knew.

That which will one day be normal sight is today called vision, sparked by the pressures of the so-called 'realistic', or contemporary; and before the new world it will *nearly* be mad not to conform— something that Hitler had up his sleeve, and certainly in his colossal brainlessness. Our psychiatrists are well on the way to manufacturing reach-me-downs of normality; the pattern was cut from a profound and gloomy stare in the mirror. Observe the fandangoes of 'personality analysis' facing the poor wretches who wish to be enthralled into gainful occupations in the United States. That is an omen: of human breakdown. The other omen is the patented solubility of intellect in the soup of the feeling of virtue: Moral Rearmament. But in the end is the beginning. That part of man called God is to be thanked for this. It is high time for Him to be brought back into the human family; He wastes our time in exile.

9

Bob Owen

OUR naive discovery that Russian education is 'ideologically loaded' will, a little later, introduce us to the idea that ours is similarly blessed; that non-ideological education, like non-ideological thought and action, is impossible. In England a good alibi for intellectual enquiry has always been scholarship; another is a worship of science; another is religion; others are careerism, self-sacrifice, murder, etc. But, in the narrower sense, we can say that fact-fetishism has always been the aim of anti-intellectual education. It is slowly giving way to enquiry, to the need to animate facts by discovering contexts. But the signs of a backward culture will include fact-fetishism, for so long the backbone of British mysticism ('the sense of reality'). A fact is the favourite coffin of an English brain; which is why British imagination has so often adopted posthumous forms.

The tendency in Wales has of course been the same. Especially elementary education consisted mostly in memorizing; a fatal association established between knowledge and intelligence, which still prevails.

'Fact-fetishism' creates a dehydrated 'reality', the sap of which is then gasified and called divine. The Welsh have most noticeably in their culture dealt in separate entities of real and super-real (divine, poetic, etc.). Hence their curious blindness to colour and building (if possible, their—perhaps *acquired*—colour sense (when one considers what remains of their crafts, woollens and the rest) seems worse than the early twentieth-, late nineteenth-century English: a relative, no doubt, and a tendency to rhetoric in their literature. Rhetoric would also be explained by the fact that, in today's world, Welsh is not exactly a living, though it remains a spoken, language. Hence its sound is more than its living sense; perhaps a language dies, as it was born, in song.

These ungracious preliminaries are an attempt to explain to myself why Bob Owen,[1] Croesor's best-known inhabitant, didn't become what he so strongly suggests he should be: a poet. Having thought this as soon as I met him, I was pleased to see that in the Williams-Ellis's *Headlong Hall* he appears as 'the Bard'. But he is not, in effect, a poet, but a bibliophile and historian known throughout Wales (and in the United States). He has written little, but is widely consulted as an authority on Welsh history by students and historians. Among his special interests are the histories of the Welsh in the United States, Mormons in Wales, the Quakers. His library is well known. It certainly suited the *tasters* of the contemporary democratic ethos to have (in the thirties), as the Press then announced, a 'quarryman' honoured with an honorary M.A., possessed of a large and quite valuable library, etc.; now the wonder seems a trifle patronizing, and not very sound. The tributes were not *just* to the obvious struggle required of a 'quarryman' (actually a clerk to the quarry company) to 'educate' himself; they partook of a monkey-typing admiration. And, of course, their implicit political nuance was: how sensible of every working man to 'better' himself individually, instead of associating in dangerous numbers for dangerous purposes (this was in 1931). Would they approve the logical development of this ethos, in Sillitoe's *Saturday Night*? As the integrity of the middle classes has been individual, so that of the working classes is collective: and perhaps never the twain shall bleat together.

Anyway, Bob Owen had indeed done all that was said of him. Democracy's great voice, *John Bull* (sounding often like a snake in the grass), wrote:

'Dear Sir,

I admire the splendid spirit and complete disregard for circumstances which prompted you, an unemployed quarryman, to cultivate a taste for literature and rare books. It is pleasing to hear that the University of Wales has decided to reward your

[1] Bob Owen died in May, 1962, aged 77.

services to Welsh bibliography by an honorary degree of Master
of Arts. I hope the University will go a little further and find you a
worthwhile position. It will never regret it. Men of your stamp
always earn their pay.'

This rather hideous backslap is, roughly, more or less representative
of the general and Press attitude to Bob's achievements, and can't
really have been too good for him, if he took it seriously. Note that
the celebrated journalistic Voice admired Bob's 'complete disregard
for circumstances which prompted you', etc. It may unhappily have
been true that to too great an extent Bob's cultural interest *was* developed against his circumstances; had it co-operated more with them, he
would, no doubt, have been a poet. But, in conformity with the kind
of educational outlook mentioned, Bob cleared out of the contemporary world into the facts of history, bringing back his considerable
spoils for our factual enlightenment. It's certainly invidious to regret
that a historian instead of a John Clare came out of Bob's experience;
yet mayn't one regret the fact that this so very interesting experience
has, in effect, no expression at all? Generally, the mind of the autodidact is kinder to the free expression of talent or genius; an academ-
ically educated Lawrence or Gorki would be something very different
from those writers. The autodidact, like the rest of us, has of course no
choice; yet it seems to me to be a partial waste that scholarship and not
creation came from Bob's experience; still, his book-collecting might
qualify under the latter category.

He grew up fatherless, perhaps deprived, with his grandmother
Ann Owen from Anglesey. He describes her as being 'small, stout,
very talkative and neighbourly'. She was the daughter of a weaver.
She could make yeast from hops, pickles and ketchup and herb drinks,
and 'there was none to beat her for salting a pig. Two pigs were used
each year.' This was in a small cottage in Llanfrothen, about forty
minutes' walk from Croesor. It was whitewashed, one-storeyed, with
living-room and bedroom containing two four-poster beds. There was
a flower garden in front and the pigsty at one end, and was locally
known as *Twll Wenci*, or The Weasel's Nest, and Bob as Little Robin
of the Weasel's Nest, which he says he didn't like. Ann Owen was a

widow when Bob went to stay with her; her four brothers had
emigrated to America in 1844. Bob, who is now seventy-five, would
thus have been with her in approximately 1895–1905. Bob's upbringing
was in part paid for by the Americans.

The Bible and the birch attended his upbringing; Mrs. Owen was
kindly but strict. At three he went to school at Garreg, the contiguous
village. He still curses the kind of education from which he there
partly suffered, other aspects of which he enjoyed. 'The British
Empire,' he says, 'was the first and foremost subject. . . . We learned
nothing about America or about Wales, but had to memorize dates
and details about the "Great British Empire" . . . we knew more about
the mountains of England and her lakes than about the mountains and
beauty spots of Wales. I could name nearly every capital of every
country in the world, but was never told about the height of Snowdon
or of the other peaks . . . the poetry that was thrust down our throats
was that of some third-rate English poets which, luckily, I have long
ago forgotten.'

He was, of course, taught in English, though there were then no
English people living in Llanfrothen (this district still being almost
entirely Welsh-speaking). 'I can remember saying my prayers in
English, although I did not understand a word.' But school had its
pleasanter side. One Hugh Hughes was a master to whom Bob became
very attached, in spite of the master's propensity for starting and
encouraging fights among the boys. Bob hated fighting, and was
small; but he did very well on the few occasions when goaded into it.
Swearing among the boys was punished with severe birchings (swearing being much worse than fighting!). 'After being spanked the
children were made to stand on one leg in a corner, or put inside a
book cupboard.' There seems to have been quite a deal of beating.

At thirteen he left school to take up work as a labourer at
Brondanw. There he was paid £2 10s. for six months' work. After a
season he was hired out to another farm for £3 for six months, with
food. Here he learned to smoke: 'There were several very interesting
people living at Cefn Kyffin in those days, and they were responsible
for introducing me to tobacco. They gave me some shag to chew,'
which turned him green. He smokes Woodbines with a birdlike

elegance; if possible, when lecturing. 'I can talk or lecture at the top of my voice'—which is at a considerable altitude—'if allowed to smoke, for two hours on end; and keep a conversation going again until midnight if my host happens to be a convivial one.'

At the farm he rose at half past five to work two hours before breakfast; he liked looking after the sheep, whose walks here extend to the tops of the mountains.

In 1900 he left the farm, engaged himself to 'one called Evan Williams of Ty Newydd Rhyd, a very eminent Biblical scholar', when Bob himself was about sixteen. His work with Evan Williams gave him a horror of horses, which he fears even more than bulls. He had a fierce temper, once exercised when a maid emptied the contents of her chamber-pot over him, a maid 'whom I had often teased'. He developed a fellow feeling for two poachers, one of whom made a habit of ducking the policeman who chased him. He moved to another farm owned by a connection of the Lloyd Georges; he became a friend of the politician later, and much admired him. The food was excellent here, especially 'the stew which we call "lobscows" was famous for its richness and high meat potency. . . . We labourers slept in a loft above the stable. It was divided in two, one loft to house the boys and the other part used as a granary where oats, barley and wheat were kept in huge oak chests mellowed almost black with age.' There were rats and 'we had a good deal of merriment when we set the cats loose in the granary. I, being a shepherd lad and anxious to make a little extra money, used to skin all the dead lambs and other animals and try to cure them before selling them to the tannery.' Snow entered through the roof-slates in winter, and 'we often woke up to find a quilt of snow on our beds . . . to dry our wet clothes we had to rely on the heat of the horses underneath us. It isn't therefore to be wondered at that so many of us (including myself) are crippled with arthritis and rheumatism. It was a hard life indeed and many today suffer from the treatment they received in those days.'

Someone noted Bob's phenomenal memory and passion for mathematics, and helped to get him a job as clerk to the local quarry company, a position he held for thirty years. Some of this time he attended night school. In those days, Bob points out, the cultural life

Bob Owen

of the valley was richer than it is today. There were innumerable choral competitions, in which the singing was, compared with today's, very good indeed; Bob thinks little of the present-day singing in Croesor. There were recitations, literary discussions, both in the village and in the 'barracks' up on the mountainside where the men lived during the working week, taking up their food and necessities from Penrhyndeudraeth or Croesor, etc. But the quarry closed in 1930, which dates the beginning of the decline of Croesor. In our broadcast Bob told us how he was deputed by the manager ('not available') to tell the men, one Saturday, that there would be no more work for them; the first and only intimation they had had of this catastrophic news. Bob was thus unemployed. But his self-education bore fruit, and his book-collecting brought him some money. In the *Daily Express* of 1931 (December 21st) we read, as mentioned: 'M.A. degree for a quarryman. Collector of 18,000 rare books.' The books may now have reached 47,000, and are to be found in almost every room in his house, including the kitchen, just above some jars, etc. This is quite a passion with him. In fact he left his wife on their honeymoon at Aberystwyth to fetch books from Carmarthen. In the thirties he frequently broadcast, and has done so frequently since. He also appears in various brains trusts, on radio and television; but has managed to escape the grimmer chores of being a 'personality'. The *Dispatch* of thirty years ago described him as 'a short man with flashing eyes of irresistible attraction'. The eyes still flash, still are imbued with a piercing clarity and good humour utterly devoid of cynicism or rancour from any sense of having spent a misdirected life; a rare creature, one who is and has been happy, still enjoys and life, looks back upon it as an exhilarating adventure. It is this clarity and this humour that so set him apart; it has the freshness, the wonderful cleanliness of the local mountain air, sane and exhilarating to be with. As in some ways his opposite, I've tried to absorb this impression he has given me of having completely escaped the psychic pock-marks of our age, its sickly *angsts*, its awful lack of elementary mental health and a *sane* love of life.

Though he is the deacon of the chapel, one couldn't quite call him 'conformist' in everything. In any case he has missed the present

H

alignments. He speaks rather vaguely against hypocrisy, but seems to consider a working minimum. 'We are all hypocrites,' he told me. The difficulty, however, is partly linguistic, I think. To be shocking is something so tritely standardized in Wales, as in provincial England; forgetting, one can be thunderstruck by what some consider to be 'frank'—the *Chatterley* case introduced us to some Establishment troglodytes. Bob belongs to the generation that found 'drama' in all this. That age is past; though the British Isles may be 90 per cent anachronistic, fulminations are not, by mere quantity, made topical. Most 'Expressed' drama is intellectually a hundred years old at least.

Bob is good about punishment; he can't believe that God could be bothered to punish, or so I understand him. He has strong feelings about illegitimacy, another prejudice not quite dead in mental and geographical provinces. He is extraordinarily permissive, quite unlike some aspects of Methodism with which we're familiar. He's a fairly keen anti-Puritan, but finds few (or no) allies in Croesor. He thinks the world has improved in his lifetime—better education, less humbug, more toleration. His attitude to knowledge is, as I have said, naive, a little like an artist's towards what was once called beauty. He collects and disseminates it without attempting to find a philosophical pattern; I think he loves it, and I know that it excites him. He is not exploitative about this at all; he regards himself as a useful functionary, which of course he is. He is quite extraordinarily not the self-made man, though he likes recognition, naturally enough. He was very pleased about the O.B.E., though I gather that some Welsh Nationalist associates were not. But an honour is an honour, and it was quite unsought, and it came from work that he loved to do: a sun-hat for a gardener?

Finally he thinks the world is slowly leaving behind its barbaric infancy. Like Maxim Gorky, he believes we're at the brink of civilization, though he realizes that many people think we have already arrived: such people, he would agree, are fairly dangerous.

He's a tiny man, with a child's candour, a warlock's shrewdness, and a poet's entrancement with all living things. But I think he owes very much the continued possession of these attributes to his wife. She is a marvellous guardian from all things harmful; Mrs. Blake must have resembled her.

10

Where Croesor Meets the World

THOUGH Bob Owen is well known, he belongs to Croesor. Though a very sociable man, who loves good company and conversation, there are aspects of him that keep him as out of 'the world' as do comparable aspects of this village. Even Merioneth is not quite the home of his spirit; he says: 'I am not loved in Merioneth.' Due, he explains, to certain opinions he holds. There was a period when he suffered considerably at the hands of the moralists, about which he says little; and he feels strongly against respectable sinners. He even disapproves of people 'marrying for lust', having a high regard for the personal or spiritual elements in marriage. On the radio he remarks upon some expressions being censored. His speech is apt to be demotic when he's excited. He remembers some Welsh preachers as being 'great sinners, drunken and dissolute men', with, nevertheless, a great gift of preaching. From this he has come to observe that great talent does not always accompany moral eminence; a subversive idea, no doubt, in Wales as in provincial England—in Methodist circles, anyway. He is positive in his literary tastes; he does not like John Bunyan, and says of Milton that he was 'in the air, not with us'. It is a not surprising fact that very social men tend to be retiring, and prefer quiet places to constant 'society'; for 'society' is not, they have discovered, very social. Bob is a shy and a deservedly well-protected man; because he has a child's delight in showing what he knows (in children miscalled exhibitionism; actually the joy of offering), he is safest in seclusion. In the world people are a little harder, a little brassier, than Bob Owen. One look at him, and another at Croesor, will show that he is in the right place.

But, of course, the world meets Croesor on some common boundary. I think the Brondanw Arms is on this boundary; Croesor and the world meet there.

It is coming down from Croesor that one is reminded of a very old description of the world, of what happens in it; a description of its decline from an older, if mythical, state of wisdom. Entering the world at the Brondanw Arms in summer, when the world is present in force in that charming pub, we can consider the following from the *Tao*:

'When the great Way declines, there is "humanity and "justice".'

And:

'Superior virtue never asserts its virtue; therefore it has virtue.
Inferior virtue never abandons its virtue; therefore it has no virtue.
Superior virtue neither acts nor aims.
Inferior virtue acts and aims.
Superior humanity acts but aims not.
Superior justice acts and aims.'

And:

'Thus, once the Way is abandoned, thereafter Virtue is asserted; once Virtue is abandoned, thereafter humanity is asserted; once humanity is abandoned, thereafter justice is asserted; once justice is abandoned, thereafter ritual conduct is asserted.

Now ritual conduct is the thin shell of loyalty and good faith and the beginning of disorder. Foreknowledge is but a blossom of the way and the beginning of folly.'[1]

'Ritual conduct'? There's less of it in Croesor: what is it? I fear, perhaps not as bad as I fear, it is the 'other-directed' mode of the 'Lonely Crowd'; allowing that behaviour must develop in cycles of

[1] *Tao Te Ching*, trans. J. J. L. Duyvendak (John Murray).

individuation and standardization, of microcosmic essence become macrocosmic atmosphere, 'ritual behaviour' is the standardization of past individuations. Certainly that which opposes 'ritual behaviour' may be pseudo-individuality, the originality that has become the cliché of our times. The *Tao*, of course, never proposes opposition of this kind. It's possible, for instance, that Thomas's drinking was an attempt to shift out of the coils of gathering 'originality' imposed upon him by his vampire appreciators. A sad man, being original in ways other than the sensationally 'different': a pity there was none competent to guard his simplicity. Originality, once known of oneself, is in these vulgar times the end of oneself; for safety, conformity outside will guard originality within; will even be the proper mode of its expression, though not *what* is expressed (Brecht). Otherwise one would end up on the Philistine's dinner-plate.

Yet 'ritual conduct' is wearing, is ungainly, is intellectually insulting and aesthetically painful. No; it is probably not the macrocosmic atmospherization of the microcosmic essence; it is just plain ashes of life. It is the smoke of ashfires created by fate's impatient urination on them—acrid, blinding and stinking. Its vehicles are, as ever before, fringers on art worlds. We behold the tics of 'creativity', the bosky but still prattling nuances of significances that have not changed (I know) much for thirty years. In a word, we have the wandering friars of 'creativity', as offered by a society without community, and who try to substitute 'creativity' for the missing familiar; society is a ballroom for the execution of quadrilles, and of those who won't dance. I never danced, but fear enabled me to represent a jig.

It would not be quite correct to represent the Brondanw Arms as such a ballroom; but on lovely summer days, when 'Time let me play and be/Golden in the mercy of his means', it is electrically contracting to be pronged up on Hampstead polemics, entering from the sun.

I've suggested that when Puritanism experiences a steep decline in its rigid standards without an accompanying alteration in social forms to employ such released energies, something much poorer, much unhappier, would result; the sordidness, the gnashed *brio*, the epileptic and cerebrating hilarity of the miniaturely damned of London acquaintance. Were the young able to be released from their hypnotized sense of the importance of the rigid absolutes against which they 'rebel', their rebellion would be enduring and useful. As it is, they sustain by opposition in a degree of sincerity and seriousness which is so little merited by the Establishment as to become its, the Establishment's, main form of nourishment; as it may come about that the lean-to shed eventually supports the old wall. It must be hinted (for this to be an at all adequate record of experience in this odd village) that the descent into the Brondanw Arms' summertime emancipation is something of a descent into the secondhand department of experience; much-used old garments, from deplorably familiar stores, are evident. We may hear, if we are sensibly attentive, that especial drone in the voice that, technically, is the enwrapping of potential opposition made possible by over-familiarity with the statement and the arguments it produces. One may sense the organized short-circuiting of communication from the inertia produced by over-familiarity; an enemy will click the hunting spears into fearsome alignment, however: having insufficient in common (just like a Great Nation) they have resonantly everything against one not partaking of the gruel of their conspiracy.

These objections, I know, are local, very personal; they mean much to me. Provided one's standards of beauty are truly one's own, the aesthetic impression of people is the most important one.

On the other hand, there is at no time in the Brondanw Arms that ritual exchange between 'locals' and foreigners, precisely formulated in terms of equality by the latter that are best calculated to preserve their sense of superiority. In Suffolk it was in part this neo-bucolic jollity that made me leave; for the cynical purposes, the Suffolk 'locals' loved to indulge in it. Wales is blessed by as great as possible an absence of class feeling as one could well expect in this society. The people have an elegance of spirit that, if so rare a matter were debased into competitive terms, would certainly make them the 'superior' of the English, who so lack this *élan vital*. So the two parties in the pub in summer appear to have worked out a very nice technique, not only of mutual toleration but, here and there, of friendship.

In front of 'the working classes' (a large section of whose incomes is greater than mine) I have always felt exiled from something more than just that, which made me feel that they were 'more' than just that. After all, my first three years were spent with them, in France, and the happy years of my childhood were those working-class friendships. They lack the cruel competitive streak of other classes, and the dingy and narrow qualities that follow therefrom. They lack delusions of grandeur, they lack the mucky psychic molasses of solitude, grandiloquent solitude; they telephone God, in this exalting conspiracy, less frequently than their 'superiors'. They're still the repository of all that's human and, in spite of present trends and fashions, appear to me to be prototypical of a new civilization. To me they represent, and have always represented, sanity: of the non-precarious kind. Day Lewis's lines (anent a feeling of being 'small' *vis-à-vis* working classes) have been much laughed at (by himself too, probably): however, they're authentic. Insubstantiality is the common feeling, protected by manners of equality veiling intentions of superiority, of the upper classes confronting the working classes; naturally, because working maintains the integration of all parts of the human being. Middle-class people work, certainly: far more competitively, far more privately, and from a psychic platform threatening constant topples. It is informing to compare this working-class substance (which Richard Hoggart suggests is being undermined by new class movements) with the near-neurotic insubstantiality of the 'new' middle—from the cruder hero of Braine to the slicker, but basically similar, ones of Amis. Vulgarity is so small a word for these as to be, in effect, a bath-towel hiding graver deficiencies. It is appalling to have to witness the attempt, since the war, of the creation of a whole scale of values based upon such meretricious and empty conceptions. The summertime Brondanw Arms holds all three classes. Like birds of different species, they just hold the same wire; but communication's lines are sometimes bent to avoid collision.

The socially falling or fallen are in better case than the 'risers'. I in the second generation, Christopher Wordsworth in the first, have a good chance of meeting terra firma; those who rise risk concussion when their heads meet the ceiling of possibility. Christopher Wordsworth was, I thought, the most noticeable person in the Brondanw Arms. I think he does this himself, in order to hide a less obvious self.

He's extremely successful; the less obvious self is one of almost celibate pedantry, rigid standards. Like me, he is deficient in the recognition of the equal reality of others; but he believes in that reality on a principle (I doubt that he has seen it clearly enough to dispense with the principle). He is one of those men whose bright and witty public personalities disguise a homely plainness (I really believe Oscar Wilde had a trace of this plainness; his decoration is otherwise unaccountable). He is oblique in communication, finding it difficult to stand still for long in the eye of any beholder. He doubts the beholder's powers of true vision, I think; he has a secret, but not a guilty one. His status (social) has for long been that of 'gentleman labourer'; he described himself to me as a ploughboy *manqué*; his physique might suggest something, not everything, of this. It has a touch of the Neanderthal—head buried down in hunched, broad shoulders; long arms. The eyes are fairly inscrutable, something of the ram's glazed immunity to the perception of others that so characterized the face of his ancestor, William Wordsworth. He is a homely, love-seeking person in the perhaps defiant garb of a nonconformist. I suggested to him that as a Tory 'outsider' he should make quite a good living as a writer; his talent (and wit) is quite evident, in Toynbee's symposium *Underdogs*.[1]

Christopher came down here eight years ago with Jeremy Brooks, the novelist and critic, to complete a novel, which remains uncompleted. 'I fell in love with the landscape,' he said. He fits well into it, and into the population. Of all the local 'foreigners', I think he has most of a quite obvious simplicity that's the main key for contentment here. His guile is an extension of this simplicity, not its contradiction; and it is not a very profound guile. But his simplicity may be a little more clever.

Over the variety integrally presides Mr. Jack Jones and his wife Nellie. Jack Jones is a vitally compact small Welshman, with a dark-bright eye whose centre, in the manner of many of his countrymen's eyes, seems to be split into bright fragments; however much you look at it, it will more be looking at you, and seeing rather precisely what you, for some reason of caution, do not see in yourself. It is an eye

[1] Weidenfeld & Nicholson, 1961.

with the Celtic hauteur of the Welsh, very fine, finely arched, this side (just) of wildness. He tends to an engineer's view of the life of his parlour; but he is not as simple, or as orientated, as he may think. He reminds one of what Gertrude Stein said of the Spanish, that they were abstract. They perceive soul spread on human bread, not always well covering it. His tones are so ringingly convivial as almost sardonically to suggest something other; one feels that his sense of humour would be best aroused at a funeral. He experiences, anyway, periodically in his parlour the funeral of certain illusions that he takes great pleasure in finding buried; for he is, now, a man of certainties. In another context he might well have been the playboy of the Western world.

Like all pubs, the Brondanw Arms is partly a waiting-room, where one might a lifetime wait for Godot, and eventually see him enter as one died out. In contrast, Suffolk pubs are parlours celebrating, if so lively a word can be used in connection with such furnished paralysis, The End. The 'Arms' cheers on the continuity. The Celt quite clearly endures, with wonderful flexibility and an interesting future.

The Brondanw Arms is a gentle introduction to the world over the border; and the world, as we stay longer in Croesor, will of course slowly percolate in; but there's not much of the world's staple diet— plump drama—for it to stay happily here. Croesor is wise enough not to oppose the world; it has never been engaged to it.

II

The Guardian of Amenity

THE beauties of North Wales have long been famous in England. In 'Snowdonia', Mr. Clough Williams-Ellis's contribution to *Britain's National Parks*,[1] the author quotes an eighteenth-century visitor's comment upon the Aberglaslyn Pass (about two miles from Croesor):

> 'How shall I express my feelings! The dark tremendous precipices, the rapid river roaring over disjoined rocks, black caverns, and issuing cataracts; all serve to make this the noblest specimen of the Finely Horrid the eye can possibly behold: the Poet has not described, nor the Painter pictured so gloomy a retreat, 'tis the last Approach to the mansion of Pluto through the regions of Despair.'

So was the effect of brilliant vitality, like diamonds pouring through a cathedral-sized jeweller's shop, upon the confined precincts of an 'ordered' (ultra-domesticated) eighteenth-century mind; it reached to the depths above which the rational tight-rope swung, evidently. This high-blood-pressure sense of 'drama', in different forms, is still with the English; we have the favoured epithets of literary journalism to point it—'passionate', 'stark', 'merciless', 'brutal', 'vicious', etc.; all relishes of 'awfulness' and violence as proper condiments of the national dish currently termed 'realism'. How sentimental! Williams-Ellis's reply to his quotation is apt; he has, he says, shot the 'issuing cataracts' in a canoe with his children aboard, and thereby applied a Welsh leech to Saxon 'passion', which was, and is, the passion of repression, moved

[1] *Britain's National Parks*, ed. H. M. Abrahams (Country Life, 1959).

122

by anything in proper motion to, I believe, improper commotion. Even Showell Styles, who takes life calmly enough, employed the Glaslyn as clothes-horses for his hero's subterranean feelings. Were I a poet, I would employ them to point to me my inhibited desire to knit woollens—the rhythms are suitable—or to dance.

Shooting the Glaslyn rapids in a canoe will serve as an analogy of Clough Williams-Ellis's witty refreshment of eighteenth-century architecture; the deliriously profound can be made to dance.

A brief consideration of the history of Nature pressed into the metaphorical service of industrially dished man will help to plot the value both of Croesor and of Clough Williams-Ellis's services as the guardian of its amenities, and of amenities elsewhere in the British Isles; we shall find a straightforward development of the melodramatic concept of Nature as a sort of super-egoist embalmer of man's bad conscience and ruined nerves into the modern view of natural beauty as an essential therapy.

A 'poetical' account (by which we mean an inexact one; an *unconsciously* symbolical one) has long been with us. The call for freed passion in Wordsworth still moves us . . . to remember that the call was not accepted as this, but subsumed into a pantheistic idealism so eerie as to be, in effect, a shy knock at death's door; the manufacturer would have opened it, had it been loud enough. It became in the character of poets of this kind not to want what they asked for, because they were trapped in an unconscious symbolism to which the key was not as Freudian as, for a while, it was hoped. The nature of 'poetical' poetry (how poetical is demonstrated by Wordsworth's failed endeavour formally to correct it) is characterized by its deracination of metaphor from a thus dichotomized reality; a tendency reaching its apotheosis in surrealism which, however, being ineffectual in England, didn't cure English poetry of this deracinated metaphoricism. But the point is that the ineffectuality of the protest—the 'poetical' protest—against industrialism is both guaranteed and served by this metaphoricism, which is the same as the metaphoricism of religion for similar purposes. Eventually 'Nature' was applied to the Caliban face with a powder-puff. Even industrialists moved into the country. In the cities there began that romanticism of the sordid in Dickens that flowered best abroad in Baudelaire, even in Celine later; the 'beauty' of squalor; beautiful to the amorous suicide, so immense a part of recent literature. Beauty proper had been internalized since the Renaissance, for lack both of outer sustenance and social health. And (as in Graham Greene) the internalized 'psychic' beauty feeds unctuously on the socially sordid.

One delighted in 'Nature' but one lived on industry; there lay the guts of life. So Nature wasn't taken seriously (only worshipfully) until the diseases consequent upon ignoring the absolute *necessity* of all that makes beauty in life became apparent; industrial efficiency seemed to demand beauty, in the form of better health through better housing, medical services, social planning, etc.: beauty and Nature came back on a scientific and self-interested basis. Of course the choric soul of beauty—the living nucleus, the attracting centre of life—cannot be found thus; hence, such beauty as we have, in a straightforward, representational, pleasant fashion, tends to thinness, lacks a dimension; in its 'advanced' forms of art is still either quite abstract or the romanticism of the ugly. For the filings of reality to configure into beauty in art, we need the magnet of a co-operative social purpose: that which once, in abstraction, was known as soul, and which imminently is to become body: but a hesitancy before the final fleshening of the word has long been noticeable.

Every item of psychic misery has its 'outer' parent, the boss who plants the super-ego to draw his 'soul'. 'Inner' is the guilt-laden hallucination of spontaneous self-generation (with perhaps God as the laboratory), productive of that dotty kind of self-responsibility upon which the majesty of criminal law depends; and that hallucination is exorcized only by increasing awareness of how man is made: to wit, by man through environment. *That* begins to make the responsibility collective; and *that* is the dawn of the civilized attitude to civilization.

Wilde's basic immorality lay in his belief in the importance of beauty, and in the implicit suggestion that beauty was the therapy of man's ills; he ran full tilt against the worship of ugliness in the guise (Victorian) of functional (profit-produced) reality. The hymnal tone in an Englishman's discussion of reality is still remarkable. Being a pioneer (much more serious—and intelligent—than his near supporters, the Pre-Raphaelites, whose look was still deliriously backward and metaphorical), homosexuality helped, being the short-circuit discipline of such a cult: i.e. being beautiful alone through lack of social support. His genius lay in his serious adoption of an aesthetic attitude to life and to humanity; ultimately, the aesthetic is the true standard, which all other standards serve. All the vices in the long run (I mean the true, not the moralistic, vices) are to be condemned because of inefficiency, because of their death-orientation; efficiency is the *mode* of beauty; and beauty is sanity triumphant, not the holy ghost of it, but the soul materialized. From Wilde's (unhappily still too implicit) philosophy to town planning and socialism is not a great step; it is a reasonable development. The day may come when aestheticism in the British Isles will not be compelled into affectation, or made a homosexual conspiracy. We can take (to parody Lenin) one step back to Keats and two forward to socialism.

However, they 'got' Wilde; they must have itched frightfully at finding the 'immoral' so beautiful. They put him out, they put their Boer War on, and their other wars. The reduction to their own absurdity was a little too evident after their First World War; the path of its bullets from *laissez-faire* ugliness to murder was a little too direct to escape intelligent observation and popular suspicion. Ugliness as the mother of violence came into the public consideration; dying apart or living together became true alternatives. Living together meant, ultimately, the resurrection or creation of beauty; beauty in social relations, in economic efficiency, in creation of environment, in creation of man. Men were ruder than their machines, whose beautiful efficiency was in danger of that repeated abstraction from human application that had, for so long, been the religious fate of human genius. But we had the sociology of the Webbs and the economics of the Marxists; a new mode of the manners that could make man had arrived; not manners gained in a series of obstacle races ('life') to posthumous perfection, but manners on a scientific (aesthetic) basis. To be rude henceforth one had to be more of a charlatan and crook; one had to be a Hitler. The challenge was, of course, accepted, man being as resourceful in wickedness as he is inspired in goodness.

Challenging thinkers and apostles of free enterprise are lively; they will soon be epileptic.

But the First World War was, indeed, the great divide; disillusionment in the Second was but a gamey recapitulation, a *modiste*, pretty uncreative echo. The First World War provided such a shocking materialization of the soul of proud man individually enterprising: the materialization of the battlefields and the ruined cities. The ruined cities of the Second World War merely started up a generation of pseudo-aesthetic vampires, the fashionable *angst*-merchants, the rhetorical despair merchants. Also, of course, the usual greasy moderators.

A little lyric of, I think, singular importance did blossom after the Second World War: rather childish, rather timid, and rather slight, perhaps; but imbued with a love of health, a belief in at least attractiveness (an art of peace), and a sense of lively rhythm: the Festival of Britain, and the new architecture loosely associated with it; a link between its gentle and positive satire and the mood of some Brecht pieces *could* be traced; and something Chinese, also, in its sensitive balance (if not identification) of order with freedom. That new appreciation of space as the soul of building and the plastic arts (as silence, the soul of music) continues; space and silence are being sculpted anew, so as to be distinguished from rehashes of old complexities —esoteric art. It was like humanity's deep breath of relief at discovering the absence of a feared total collapse. Our age is, perhaps, the age of space—in various fields and senses. We are not dead; in our time, that is sufficient inspiration to life. After all, the Victorians were not as certain.

That we are not dead means an awakening of the sleepers at a moment of peril; one of the pioneer awakeners in his chosen field was Clough Williams-Ellis who came to town planning and amenity preservation largely through his repeated observation of the monstrous environs allowed to accrete around the few remaining architectural treasures. Post-war conditions were immediately responsible for a wave of 'new world' building and planning; at least a token gesture was desirable towards the fit-for-heroes country. But also to encourage at least the dream of a newly ordered society was the fact that industrial finance had been forced to renounce the pirate competition of the pioneering days; there must have been some measure of reflection in the wave of town planning from the gathering monopoly-grouping of capital and the growth (formally) of industrial good manners. A 'nice association of self-interest (ever England's favourite) with idealism' was gathering strength. Cadbury and others (taking their cues from America) had concluded that there might be economic good sense in clean and healthy living conditions. That the best exploitation involves a considerable degree of social welfare tempts some (who need no tempting) to conclude that capitalism is humanitarian; limits of social welfare are always evident to dispel such sentimentality. However that may be, social welfare in two bursts, after two wars, brought in tow with it town planning and, of course, artistic revivals. The ethos ultimately inimical to this enlightened capitalism was distillable from its overt recognition of the vital role of conditioning (through environment) in human development; this had, previously, been a socialist idea, and called historical determinism.

Once the factor of conditioning is allowed the whole ethics of self-responsibility in anarchic and competitive society crumble; the life of the body, and of the mind and soul as part of it, assumes priority. Co-operation, the engine of planning, begins to foreshadow its economic essentials. The power of the English to hold two incompatible ideas in their heads at the same time without either a short-circuiting explosion or enlightenment—the ideas of free enterprise and planning, which is specifically socialistic—no longer surprises; but makes us tired. Fortunately for Clough Williams-Ellis, town planners, and especially architects, can most freely believe in the prosecution of their work and art without feeling to any great extent politically compromised. Frank Lloyd Wright, for instance—an individualist of sometimes Nietzschean colouring (which is not the same as fascist)—could say, when he saw Moscow first after the Revolution: 'Here, indeed, is greatness; here is the future!' Which is inconsistent only on the surface; we have yet to learn that deep individualism is impossible without true community . . . without order, planning; that the biggest chunks and delicacies snapped off the individual occur in the crude clashes of private economy, that the biggest waste of genius occurs

through the energy essential to its competitive marketing. Nietzsche
and Marx are compatible. A nice fundamentalism in the architects'
attitude—deriving from the fact that they'll all need houses—carries
them along, but not the whole way in a happy a-politicism; artists are
perhaps less happily accommodated, as they're beginning to discover.
Mr. Williams-Ellis personally favours what he considers to be the
enlightened democracy of the Scandinavian countries—'well-educated
democracies—q.v. the excellent teaching of citizenship in their schools
. . . much of our education is ill-directed and we are too afraid of
discipline which, however, at our present low level of aesthetic
consciousness it may be just as well to have no more'. I fear that he
does not see the soul of man, in its positive and non-escapist connotation, as the essence of his economy. 'By their fruits ye shall know
them' means, however, that a man is what he does—how he lives,
what he does to live, the social patterns created by what he does and
how he does it.

Because, through a long (400-year-old) family connection with this
district, he has managed to eschew that kind of 'bright' individualism
whose inner resource is its outer competitive power, he is an individual
whom we may call 'vintage'; laid down long ago, not of the slight and
theatrically bitter kind who scrabbles to the room at the top. Hence
he can properly possess a social consciousness: it is probably this kind
of social consciousness that has made socialism less characteristically
necessary to him. That such individuals verge on eccentricity—they
are not with the new brotherhoods either of competition or of
socialism—and may wear certain techniques of slightly farouche
isolation is inevitable; that isolation will also allow the better brewing
and consolidation of their art, from a depth of contemplation. His self-
definition away from his fellow men is a constant, unpremeditated
activity. In a Welshman it also all the more means 'uncapturedness'
(not untamedness; uncaptured does not mean uncivilized). His pride
is inbuilt, expressed as an allergy to the kind of 'democratic' familiarity
whose main intention is often, I believe, the annihilation of quality—
the egalitarianism that poses as the love of equality. Whereas i
equality is a fact, standardization is inimical to it. He has a quality of
bright absence (which is particularly Welsh) as opposed to evasive

absent-mindedness. Where you are, he probably is not; that is not to infer that he is spaciously and speciously nowhere (the other day he was busily tidying up a grotto near his house). His walk, his straight and flexible physique, are in this character. He is so well cut for the environment as to have no invidious interest in any but an aesthetic relationship with it: the French have this; the lugubrious sentimentality of Saxons arises much from their incomplete detachment from their grey world, hence the equivocation of their philosophy and their perception of it. Lawrence writing of the Etruscans beautifully described (and none but he has done this) the blithe distinction of such natural objectivity; it gave their art the Blake line. To be semi-detached from environment (here, the gruel of patriotism, its chauvinism) is empathetically to participate in a sort of necrophilic life with it.

A biologically cunning man, Clough held this quality of positive and creative separation, and furnished it with the *techniques* of aesthetic sensibility so markedly more developed in English than in Welsh culture. His rebellion was thus ultra-personal and characteristic, a matter of clearing the ground for his own talents. 'I grew up,' he says, 'with a definite reaction against obedience, and was inclined to suspect and question orders of any sort.' For the opposite possibility, opposite both of his distinction from environment and his obedience to elders (conjoined), was expressed with unusually substantial symbolism: of the bottom of a boat he built as a child, he says: 'How voluptuously the warm pitch, soft and toffee-like, caressed and embraced the toes.' So, the distinction from environment and the rebellion against elders was motivated by an attachment to something given only a symbolical form: and what may that have been? Whatever it is, it is his attachment. Rather, the core of so abstract a nostalgia is in no way to impede, but instead to have helped create, his future-looking work. He curiously seems to me to have smuggled—or transmuted—nostalgia into future-seeking; one cannot quite distinguish it in him, or in much of his architecture. The rationalization he offers is in his appreciation of the Scandinavians again: 'The Scandinavians are not "modern" in the ruthless and revolutionary French or Dutch way, iconoclastically, violently breaking all that has gone before. They are not concerned to abolish the old forms, but to modify them. They have learned to speak

I

the old language in a crisp and vivacious fashion, adapted to a quick-
ened tempo of living that makes it seem like a new language but it is
really a stronger thing than that; it is the traditional speech of a people,
rediscovered and redeveloped.' Which is social-realist according to its
theoretical promulgation and not according to some Soviet historicism
in the arts; and (to cap the point) it is also and conversely a warning
against 'self-generated' originality and formalistic modernism well put
by Clough's friend Lewis Mumford in the latter's comment on the
U.N.O. building in New York:

> 'I will say that the Secretariat Building seems to me a superficial
> aesthetic triumph and an architectural failure. A few more triumphs
> of this nature and this particular school of modern design might
> be on the rocks.
>
> In this building, the movement that took shape in the mind of
> Le Corbusier in the early 1920's has reached a climax of *formal
> purity and functional inadequacy* [*my italics: a good definition, also, of
> contemporary individualism*]. Whereas modern architecture began
> with the true precept that form follows function, this new building
> is based on the theory that even if no symbolic purpose is served
> function should be sacrificed to form. This is a new kind of
> academicism, successful largely because its clichés readily lend
> themselves to imitation and reproduction. In the present instance
> it has brought into existence not a work of three-dimensional
> architecture but a Christmas package wrapped in Cellophane.
> Functionally, this building is an old-fashioned engine covered by a
> stream-lined hood much embellished with chromium. This package
> has been conceived with what would appear to be not even an
> industrial-stylist's interest in the contents.'[1]

Incidentally, 'This is a new kind of academicism' expresses the
burden of John Berger's polemics against 'modern art'.

True, and as suggested, Clough Williams-Ellis's appreciation of
Mumford's sound strictures, and his own devotion to the truly–
organic, progressive from traditional—modern architecture is no

---

[1] Quoted in *The Pleasures of Architecture* by C. and A. Williams-Ellis (Cape, 1954).

entire. Recalling his memories of the bottom of that boat with its soft and toffee-like pitch, wherein I discern the abstract nostalgia mentioned, one may observe both in the gardens of Plâs Brondanw and in his collection of witty follies at Portmeirion (the inspiration was Portofino) that the inert, dead material of building, and the non-human flora of the garden, strangely hood still active ghosts of an indeterminable period—suggestive, as I have said, of the Cocteau sets in *La Belle et La Bête*. Only the swiftness of the shooting of those Glaslyn rapids in his canoe made lines sharp enough ('witty') to define him from some beloved past time. And 'For as long as I live I shall remember my first sight of that lovely shell [Kirby Hall], its long, grey flanks catching the golden light of a July evening, the diamonds of the leaded casements flashing and glowing as diamonds should . . . midsummer evening glamour. . . .' With such sirens in wait, separation seemed essential; only later did he return.

He was intended for engineering, but with a certain valour eventually had his way. 'It seems to me that the great men of this world may be just those who contrive to keep the sublime valour of their childhood. They could scarcely add to it,' he writes in his autobiographical *The Architect*. Being an endemic individualist, he could support profitably his old headmaster's precepts, which were more usefully the harnesses for this opposite breed than precepts for the raising of 'democrats'.

'And what was it that he had to express, this iron-willed, soft-spoken headmaster? A belief in equal opportunities for all, in the discipline, satisfaction and usefulness of hard work, in co-operation as against competition, in education as against examination successes, the brotherhood of man as against a narrow patriotism, the service of mankind as against self-advancement, of a school of good citizens as against a small aristocracy of scholarship and a ruck of mediocrities.' (*The Architect*.)[1]

The competence of the social system to 'raise' such principles to an ethical idealism by its grey opposition makes them less interesting than

[1] Bles. 1928.

they might otherwise be; though for a public school (Oundle, the master being Sanderson) they are unusual, in that the *esprit de corps* advocated is not apparently attached to an élite. To believe in equal opportunities . . . is to believe indeed. But if we care to consider Williams-Ellis's degree of loyalty to, and application of, such principles, we would have to bear in mind the interesting naivety of his mind, eminently suitable to a dedicated architect. And we might allow this naivety the intuitive selection of properly democratic from egalitarian principles; his allergy to the latter, characteristic and practical, to the more discerning mind will show him to be an advocate of the former. As a town planner and amenity guardian, for instance, he does *not* believe in the domination of the 'average man's' taste; which, he must know, is an injection from without—like all taste but that of genius, which is a subtler amalgam. But in agreeing to the naivety of his mind, we would also (perhaps suspecting 'Welshness') have to allow for the extremely subtle rind to this naivety, allowed and nourished and even necessitated by the naivety; a rind of some strategical brilliance. In a democracy, it is astonishing how much autocracy may be smuggled in to serve that democracy, and how much egalitarianism may be smuggled in to subserve authoritarianism: the way of the world, indeed. People, oddly, know this; that Clough is locally accepted as a *Welshman*, in spite of his mainly English culture, shows the degree to which an autocratic naif may wear clothes suitable to his *native* functions.

If the ideology of painters tends to run down the canvas in terms of the constituency of their paints, architects are lucky in having their bricks made for them; unlike, also, writers, who are reduced to a life-time of brick-making for posterity to use in proper works of art. Works of art in an age of shoddy bricks are thereby affected. Bricks only go ideological when they're dropped or thrown: perhaps Clough indulged a little in this: 'Yet happiness, as is common though not universal, was what I chiefly demanded of life, not through wisdom or virtue or love, still less through riches or amusement, but through work—the work that I felt it was in me to do.' Perhaps with the advantage of a stranger's eye I can see what is inherently obvious in the proposition of happiness as an aim, which is that though happiness may have been greatly persuaded and even enjoyed in a kind of empathetic admiration, it was not quite achieved. To recapitulate three levels of a nostalgia that contradict the possession of happiness: basic, the departed spiritually, because anachronistically present physically, tonnage and solidity of the house, Plâs Brondanw; the (to me) haunted garden, wherein the ghosts of the house (it was burned in the 1950's, rebuilt recently) roam chuckling; and the lyric, not the strident statement, of Portmeirion (which is like a town in a child's heart). There is a fragrance here that may burn like incense to the old gods constituting the mortal *shell* of Clough, addressed to something much older. The shell, I mean, is built of the stone images of the gods; but that stone is but the ruin of a long-ago life. Few can be older than a Celt, because a Celt has not suffered those hiatuses of revolutionary progress; he presents a fair continuity from the historical dawn, and his beginnings are visible in his representation. I know that race—but too much on a principle used to avoid an *embarrassing* perception—is discounted as a characterizing entity; I think otherwise. He who restricts deep variety among the races of the world discounts a deeper community. Either the roots or the flowers are the same; it is not the flowers. Clough's gaze, like that of so many of his countrymen, is congenitally ruptured from its human object; his profession is sufficient rationalization, of course. ('I was, am, and ever shall be, almost imbecile in my inability to remember faces. . . .')

He is an interesting man, as I have tried to suggest, and if I write at some length about him, it is because a proper understanding of him will greatly help to explain the precise nature of the community at Croesor, and what, individually, one may hope to gain in perception of the world therefrom. For he is an enactor (rather than, as some may think, an actor) of some Zeitgeist of eternal occurrence; like a tree exploiting contemporary weather for ancient survival. So in another his gaze without such supports as I have mentioned might be paranoiac, had he not the perfected technique of the transmutation of nostalgia into contemporary art. It is the deep-rooted strength of his otherwise 'paranoid' vision that burns it free of aberrational clutterings, and re-connects past and present. Reason interrupts obsession creatively; prolongs it insanely or rhetorically.

To resume, then, a brief account of his life: he studied for a short time his chosen profession, launched out (like Lutyens) with only a rudimentary training (no doubt at the point where training began to reach conformity), and eventually became a successful architect in a style wedding eighteenth-century classicism with an element of Gothic lyricism (and/or humour) compounded into contemporary terms. The spark to ignite his love of landscape (with which town planning necessarily consorts) was, as I have said, the First World War, which confirmed in him what he already had every disposition to suspect: 'I am confirmed in my original suspicion that war is the most disastrous madness for all concerned, and my abhorrence of it has inevitably led me to take an interest and even some small part in politics.' His wife Amabel, a socialist and, like his friend Bertrand Russell, a supporter of the C.N.D. campaign, must certainly have also influenced him. He learned also the ways of the world during the war, as much as he cared or needed to: 'One was permitted, it seemed, to express pacifist views, so long as it was generally known that one had failed to live up to one's principles!' Probably he can afford the diminuendo in the principle of this discovery expressed by the exclamation mark because of other dedications already referred to. But his attitude to these 'ways of the world' is most cogently expressed (as it was by Wilde) in the near dandiness of his appearance; thus we define ourselves out of the muddier contexts of our times. His enlightenments, a slighter term than 'disillusionments', have never impeded the successful prosecution of his work, being co-ordinate and not theatrically chaos-orientated.

His passion for the preservation of amenity seems to be a personal one luckily paralleled in contemporary needs and realizations; he would in another age have been another Beckford. His feeling for beauty is particularly 'old-fashioned' (though the *avant-garde* snarls at it seem now to be approaching their desirable end; the chaos-mongering of that particular rage becomes too obviously a luxe of impotence, a sentimental indulgence in the hysterically lustful misanthropy of tired people). True, that *élan* in the wave of making great beauty is not yet present because the synthesis of political, aesthetic and intellectual principles is not yet possible; Clough has bypassed such embarrassments in ways all his own. In his *England and the Octopus*,[1] a major event in the initial onslaught on urban horrors and a brave and witty book whose value endures (I came across a review by Lawrence, approving), one may note the contemporary atmosphere in which it was written in a quotation from the great poet Rabindranath Tagore:

'Have you never felt shame when you see the trade advertisements, not only plastering the whole town with lies and exaggerations, but invading the green fields, where the peasants do their honest labour, and the hill-tops, which greet the first pure light of the morning? . . . This commercialism with its barbarity of ugly decorations is a terrible menace to all humanity, because it is setting up the ideal of power over that of perfection.'

This was said in Japan. Since then the 'barbarity of ugly decorations' has dressed in art; in an art that (to some of us) has thereby acquired an odd, demi-mondaine panache; a look not quite substantial. In *Plan for Living* Clough admonishes against 'private right to do public wrong'. He asks, in reply to those cultural levitationists who satisfy their masochism by pressing ugliness into psychic gymnastics: 'Why have an environment that needs resisting?' His general attitude to the state of the country is expressed in his comment on Sydney harbour and town: 'By God what a site! By man what a mess.'

An account of his public activities would be out of place here, and are sufficiently well known. I am concerned with his place and function at the gateway to Croesor. He is the landlord of several housing groups in the district. What is patently obvious is that Croesor and the environs owe much, indeed most, to him for their present unspoiled condition. He is in truth the guardian at the gate, and one can only hope that his care and his attitude will pass on to those who succeed him. A landlord who cares for the appearances, the amenities, of his property and sites is rare indeed; much of the uniqueness of Croesor is due to him.

There has been criticism of this role, even during my stay in the village. He has been accused of keeping 'prosperity' (industry) away

[1] Bles. 1928.

from the place. I can only hope he continues to do so, if indeed the
accusation is true. It must surely be agreed, now that the situation is
as it awfully is, that the very viability of continued 'prosperity' is
affected by the preservation of such sanctuaries as Croesor and the
lands so splendidly preserved by the National Trust and other bodies.
Even an increasing majority of industrialists begin to or actually do
realize this. *Beauty* is an economic necessity, in that large sense of
economic whereby it includes psychological harmony, spiritual well-
being and the wisdom that its presence gradually induces. *Perspective*
is the crying need of crowded man; in Merioneth we still are able to
find it; the rising incidence of mental breakdowns is the proving other
side of the coin. The *individual* pursuit of wealth is spiritually mori-
bund; because the communal enjoyment of it is progressive: *pace* the
philosophers of the *Daily Express*.

One successful campaign against such industrial intrusion waged by
Williams-Ellis was that against the erection of a hydro-electric dam
(guaranteed to produce, when completed, the equivalent of half a
day's national production of coal per annum). It would have involved
the flooding of valleys, the laying of pipes down mountain gorges, the
building of dams; with no certainty that technical obsolescence would
not have coincided with its completion. The story is told in perhaps
the wittiest production of Amabel and Clough Williams-Ellis, their
Headlong Down the Years.[1] They were opposing not so much a sound
industrial investment as, in essence, the vulgar commercial enthusiasm that masks so often nothing less than Philistine destructiveness.
In *Headlong*, as two quotations will show, the authors are curiously in
accord with another whose Marxism they would not, I understand, at
all approve. In *Headlong* we read:

> ' "This concern with the beauties of Snowdonia which has
> irritated Mr. Escot—just as I feared it would—the fuss that we
> make about open-cast mining. To us all it stands for something—
> it is real enough, but it is also a symbol."
>
> "A symbol of what?" asked Mr. Escot.
>
> "Of Feng Shui," said the Squire decisively. "Of the eternal

[1] Liverpool University Press, 1952.

harmonizing of Art with Nature. Man may—indeed must—alter Nature, but his works must not tip the balance too far. . . . Consult the genius of the Place in all," he added. "No arrogance, but an attentive eye." '

While Christopher Caudwell, in his *Further Studies in a Dying Culture* (Bodley Head, 1950), writes, in the essay 'Beauty':

'Those elements in nature which are most universal and have changed least in the history of man, may be expected to produce, in interaction with him, the most constant quality. Hence we feel rightly that there is something simple, primitive, and instinctive in the beauty we see in certain primitive, simple things . . . [but] The richest and most complex appreciation of natural beauty belongs to the civilized man, not to the primitive. . . . The ancient town, with weathered walls, full of history and character, is a part of nature, and is yet a completely artificial product; the sun lights it and the wind weathers it. *There is no dichotomy between nature and art*, only the difference between pioneers and settled inhabitants.' (My italics.)

With which we may cap a quotation from the previously mentioned authors' *The Pleasures of Architecture*:

'In architecture the work of art becomes a part of the earth in a peculiar degree, and the thought of its being "rolled around in earth's diurnal course" will never seem foreign to the architect's mind. His building will form an integral part of a sunset, a moonrise, or it will blot out a patch of stars. . . . [An architect] . . . will lie awake listening to the storm in the night and think how the rain is beating on his roofs, he will see the sun return and will think that it was for just such sunshine that his shadow-throwing mouldings were made. . . . On one side he enjoys a sense of dominance over natural forces, and on the other of partnership with them.'

Or, as the *Tao* says: 'For great carving is not done by hacking.'

Speeding lyrically in his Morris Minor, like a warlock to a coven, his journey outwardly is at one with the surmised inward journey: which is the look of an artist who has achieved his forms. His journey backward to a pristine view is also his journey forward to its establishment now.

He has offered as central to his philosophy a passage from Don Marquis. He said, at the memorial service to his friend and colleague, the late Sir Patrick Abercrombie, quoting from Don Marquis: 'Levity is the result of spiritual and aesthetic poise. A person who is groping and struggling and fighting for such poise is worried and grave. All progress is towards levity through gravity. Weight then wings! But it is the wings that are the gaol, not the weight. People who understand only weight and gravity are trivial and half-people.' True; we have it in Nietzsche's gay science, and the *Tao* has it in the wisdom of triumph through effortlessness, and the 'emptiness' of true wisdom. It is the reply to all Teutonic profundity, and it is the subtlest perception we have of the very spirit of life. In Croesor, which cleanses the soul, we view it on great days.

PART TWO

Interlude

A Touch of Death

PERHAPS with an unconscious purpose, the London congestion makes death remote and unthought of: its remoteness is partly maintained by the sensationalism with which it is treated. Sensation is the consciously indigestible. In a couple life and death return to one's awareness in Croesor where, for instance, that kind of identity consisting of a nervous wall of impressionistically nipped-off reflexes to an environment too vast and heterogeneous for sensible assimilation, departs. Life is the first to return, and his brother hovers then nearer again.

For to life attaches that fear of it formed in its romantic appreciation: *any* qualitative appreciation of a necessarily abstracted portion of life is the disguised resistance to it. A *whole* love of life is unconscious; none was more macabre than those 'life-fans' set jigging by D. H. Lawrence; none more grotesque than the many English kinds of its tasters.

Were life wholly loved, death would be unknown; for it is only known in concepts built out of resistances to life. It is *seen* happening to others, true: that isn't knowledge. Knowledge of death is always hypothetical; there's nothing to suggest, however, that concepts surrounding the non-existent state are not salaciously tinctured with . . . what? Only profounder concepts, the answer to all of which is the non-existence of the conceived condition.

But we know death in life; it is a major function of art to depict it. What relation can it bear to death? Some to the stages of the approach to death: tiredness, apathy, cynicism, hatred, destructiveness; lovelessness, supremely. And indeed the faces of men who love not, if they lust for, what they do—such as careerist politicians—die before the

141

man. Such faces become composed of a material not living flesh; they are draped. Many inhibitions will creak the creature to a near standstill; the standstill is psychically most suggested by the abstract vitality of people who, in Lawrence's terms, don't live from their 'centre' which, to complete the thought, must be identified with the centres of others: in a word, with the community.

Death in life is exile from the community; no whisky of esteemed isolation can substitute for the authentic nourishment of the community.

Life is to be experienced in one way: permissive involvement. Death in another way: compulsive involvement, or compulsive detachment. Life is when one permits for oneself; when one doesn't, death is. Permission may take on the form of a fluent and rooted purpose—it may even resemble 'letting' in the old sense, a term offering some pertinent etymological information. The opposite of permissive is obviously compulsive, less obviously that deracinating epilepsy of alleged 'vitality', a dance of the nerves today confused with joy. In effect, the dance of life is quiet, like joy; the noise of happiness is the failing and fraying perimeter of that condition. Likewise, love is eternity interrupted by thought, an excitement in temporal life.

In more detail, death is for me contained in, for example, the search for integrity by an earnest (in the mirror) artist; it is death to search for what one has, because the search is for its possession to death.

It is contained also in the abortion of human relationships by their pathological discussion.

It is contained in the murder of life by *its* pathological discussion: wherein it is hoped that the timeless, by neurasthenically punctual snipping of scissors, may be seduced into a temporality disguised as eternity.

Death has been written in most forms of liveliness; when painted, its presence is more easily apparent, the seeing eye being more intelligent than the reading eye. There is death in the surrounds of Blake's madly 'vital' life; eighteenth-century death, the Palladian, as in Flaxman's drawings, and ranted against in Fuselli's work. Life was reduced to the concentration, lustful, of a flea in order pregnantly to oppose the vast and 'imposing' (actually 'supposing') flats and elegant curves of eighteenth-century, ramifyingly bourgeois, England. This

England is analysed, by shooting a fast version of it into the twentieth century, in Brecht's *Threepenny Opera*: the same commerce of uncreative anomalies.

Whence death? Lawrence said, in the quelling of the sex. I think that is a sign, and only signally a cause.

Death is the price paid by a primitive organization for productive purposes; the even more primitive individual dies into the community; and the community thus fosters the new individual, the ground for whom is the compost made of the dead barbarians. All wild things die in organization, which leads the sentimental anarchists into the silly equation of death and organization; but death without life is impossible, and the death of the primitive is the birth of the civilized; after all, only the social analogy of the Dyonisian cult.

Sex, to tell the truth, does not 'die' in repression; and repression is or was the saving grace of the English. Without it they provide the most alarming strip-tease of all time, or at least comparable with the declining Roman Empire. Not even in repression; it creates floats upon which the dreaming mind pilots the way to heaven, which is then hauled down, by social engineers, to earth. Praise God! He is the pilot.

Nothing is wasted; the eunuch sings, the ascetic forecasts, the fascist pulls down the anachronistic prison of his times in his own ruination. But to realize this fact, that nothing is wasted, is to develop the techniques of economy; only possible because waste is not a law of life.

To confuse knowledge with action—to think that the knowledge that nothing is wasted leads to waste—is topically fallacious. Such confusion—of knowledge with action—is the hallucination born of their age-old dichotomy.

The Welsh appear not to have learned the death of ritual living; for they ride their Church with *élan*, and the relationship is very subtle and not as decently repressive as might be feared. The Welsh have not been *broken in*; they are naive in life, and may bypass the routines of approximation to death that industrialism plus racial torpor and strategical insulation in sensitivity have given the English. So, in Croesor, as an interlude between the first part and the Journal (which is a description day by day of my life here, mainly reading), I would like to attempt, in terms of paintings done by a friend of mine, to describe some elements of death which I think the Welsh, and above all the Croesorians, have escaped.

My friend is an old-fashioned representationalist who, by an odd trick of unsophistication, has avoided becoming academic and awaits, with justified confidence, the wholesale return to representationalism and the resurrection of Beauty as the primal concept of art. For in his best pictures we have that contemporary rarity: *time and space in represented forms*, which, *vis-à-vis* post-Picasso art, is the distinction of the old Masters. Picasso achieved minutes, in his early representational period, of that of which the old Masters achieved eternities. Then art killed time, and was two-dimensionally splashed, timeless and eventually spaceless (abstract), over the prostitutionally accommodating canvas, which 'took part' in (took the living part away from) the picture; which became no picture, but one of the world's objects—anti-art. (The surrealists did this honestly in *objets trouvés* and soft watches.) That is modern art's vaunted liberty: the liberation of soul from body, of metaphor from reality, of art from society and humanity; its impalement of Beauty on the especially cadavered brand of 'reality' from which such artists derive their masochistic joys.

But my friend, the old-fashioned representationalist who by that fluke of unsophistication and a somewhat over-kindled heart failed to prevent the incursion of time and space into his pictures, has his days, and years, off. Which brings me to his representation of death: a series of 'lively' portraits commissioned by an abbey.

The setting is, of course, the one we know, of a society rancid with the absence of a rational application of a properly humanistic ideal; of a society without an ideal, which therefore in its art invents one cerebration after another of that social link—man to man—missing because the cohering ideal is lost, buried under rhetorical vituperations of its unavoidable destiny: socialism.

It is the setting of the soul on the spree, the body in the grave of ritual life, the mind all *modiste* in its tipsy unhingedness, wearing its soul askew, and scrambling with its 'perceptive' eyes the beauty of the world into (as Lawrence said of what they'd done to Cézanne) 'significant form'—i.e. an insignificant leer of humanity gelded. Never before has epilepsy been confused with dancing, and profundity with chaos.

PORTRAITS OF DEATH IN SEVERAL POSES

The queer villains of his representation gazed mournfully, like un-employed milk-bar attendants, at us; hoping in us to join the life-giving battle of their existence. But we could not co-operate. These villains were adequately representative of the contemporary failure of men to move in the shrouds of their spiritual status. They proclaimed the leery death of the protagonist spirit, and the lack of birth of any-thing to follow. His Knight stood uneasily disentangling himself from a visceral tree, as from his own entrails. Upon his tinny features rested a frail leer of spiritually having put one over on somebody, but not on himself. He nearly grinned outright at his spiritual fame, as did and does D—— the artist when in that thrall. However transcendentally vague his castle might be in the distance behind him, he couldn't hide his rascally appreciation of its actual solidity: property just wouldn't, in this uneasy allegory, quite make the grade to soul. Pilloried by that spiritual accolade, the poor Knight could not move; in two dimensions, in two other pictures, he sideways scanned with mingled horror and hypocritical complacency a monk kneeling before him—rather, it was the bishop now who stood in the foreground. Between the bishop and the monk a treaty of complicity signed itself ocularly. The monk quivered as in the memory of good meals and in their creative and religiously proper anticipation. The bishop faced, with more art and craft, the need of even more cunning equations between the worlds of Caesar and God, steering so nicely between, touching in his conscious-ness neither. As cartoons depicting the hangover of Christianity they would have been successful; but their purpose, decoration of the abbey, inhibited their witty application to this theme. Doggone, they damply surveyed an immovable drop-scene of the world paralysed in their own image.

So complementarily in this game of flesh and spirit two fat ladies were made of spiritually extracted flesh, which logically became balloons of flesh; the forms of sensuality in the rubber blown up by

K

the exhausting spirit. Like their contemporary analogies, 'good women', they were vampires to fill their swollen and formal sensuality with the lives of their lovers: that has been how, for centuries, women have been 'wonderful': a poor commerce made evident in the slow and cautious equalization of the sexes.

These plastered and paralysed cartoons were dried in the dry desert of the studio, from which he was departing a little later than we. We discussed these matters at length; of the fallacy of requiring a rich emotional life for rich emotional paintings. The rich emotional life had, indeed, exhausted him; and he was thrown (a man of working-class extraction, hence defenceless against the ploys of 'sensual' spiritualists, the free-lifers of our day) perilously against the fangs of spiritual worlds, almost edible in his authentic naivety of regard. He had plumbed the depths of what I'm tempted to call 'Suffolk Art': balloons of flesh blown up by exhausting spirit; the folksy proto-substance of our day in England now. Their typical substance is dry plaster. As I, a failing poet of the thirties, wrote: '. . . there are no emotions with which to bandage the dead'. Such bandaging persists and flagellation in moments of great exasperation. Suffolk, for the foreigners, is the tomb; their art, that of the winding sheet.

The case of D——, before we leave him, can be regarded as being interestingly typical of the increasing number of working- or lower-middle-class artists. Like Lawrence, the great precursor in modern times, they are equipped with the best sensory apparatus. They are in touch with Nature and the nature of men. From that follows their first and usually insuperable obstacle: they see too much for their individualistic, commercial exploitation of it. They see the phoney inflations of class attributes as psychic or spiritual ones. They see plastered the queasy superiority of individuals as spiritual attributes, money superiority equated with spiritual superiority. They see the mean psychology of competition; and lament the sad exhalations of Nature away from this travesty of Nature. Hence they see the commercial necessity of equipping themselves with a *weltanschauung* of the many provided by the middle-class-dominated market in art. They feel forced to achieve a modish complexity; or alternatively they can acquire a still more modish simplicity. What they cannot do is to apply the complex involvements of their simple view. As long as they paint or write like children, all's well. But let them put a mature brain on the child's direct vision and all is ill; too many emperors' clothes will perish. D—— was too intelligent and too cultured to do the simple stuff. But not too naive to hanker after some favoured *angsts*. Genuine if actually unimportant in the middle classes, these are ruinous to those whose class experience makes them wholly irrelevant. The resulting neurotic complexity and frustration make life very difficult. Perhaps Henry Moore is an example of one such? So working-class artists decoct a whisky of the soul out of the simple grains of Nature; and then must learn its sales techniques. That their wide and easy world sensorily perceived with their native fluency must be shrunk for intoxicating narrowness is certain. Or was; we enter a period of directly working-class representation in the arts today, notably in the theatre. Their success depends upon the audience. That there'll be a compromise in the form of extraneous desperation isn't to be doubted. They'll have to shriek and carry on more than in real life, just to be noticed, and just to cater for the middle-class expectations of working-class vitality: vitality, dramatically, still expressing itself in carryings-on. Pent-up passion still being the only recognized form of passion: fizz of a bottled-up people. The fruits of national constipation can't be other than the obvious. Rich dirt and art still make their association.

For actually it's to be doubted that working-class art in this present context *is* working-class art; may possibly be working-class feeling expressing itself in the opera of middle-class gesture, even or especially if the aitches in speech are dropped. That the only reason for taking the working classes up a small height (to prevent their taking themselves up a dangerously greater one) is to drop them, is certain. Comic baubles of mankind; to be heard in a theatre with reverence, mark you. Reverence is in the nicest absence of a real reaction. To repeat, Brecht alone has managed this; and his characters are utterly devoid of recognizably 'working-class' carry-on: their working-class characteristic is entirely one of depth: they are characters who deal with necessity, like those of ancient Greek drama, and such as haven't been on stages for centuries, though Shakespeare and Ibsen are near.

D—— remains in a quandary; what cunning of insight he could straightly put into his portraits and landscapes! When he renounces the ancient lyricism, the pawing auto-intoxication of nature lovers, and the pseudo-exaltation of the wonder-of-the-individual school. As the individualistic armour leaks, as the jelly-man seeps through, what a visual harvest is there to be gained to lead, in a new world, to a recovery of the social-heroic view of man, the pride of the universe. Relevant, centred in the universe of space and time, the man of, again, significant thought and action.

SOME CONCLUSIONS

The Celts, who have an ancient sense of form and order (*The Book of Kells*), are the least happy and efficacious of legislators; the English and the Germans, who have the least inner sense of order, who are *par excellence* the fans of chaos, whose impassivity sometimes successfully blocks a hysteria periodically outbreaking (as yearning in Wagner) (as syrup of fig-leaves in Elgar), are the world's most efficient legislators. Each to his talent from his own provocational basis. Blake bounded the exploding brain of madness with lines of fire, which danced as none since in the triumphant endeavour; and pioneered a work with a great future: the marriage of heaven and hell, also of insanity and sanity, when society permits one to call upon the other in a parlour of suitable light. Goethe, a literary mason of genius, proved the ambiguity inherent in such solid masonry in Thomas Mann's development from him. But Shakespeare, the genius of fluidity in form, of energy in repose, neither courted failure by over-solid masonry of form, nor gave any clue to success by an inspiration less incandescent (because more hemmed in) than Blake's. He was the last whole artist, and his short-term prophecy was Doom, because his certain establishment was Progress. Shakespeare 'separates out' in Milton and Blake; Blake, by making his ambition Milton's achievement, liberated his own triumph in Shakespeare's content—abstracted by the times into the conventions of Inspiration. But he dreamed of Michelangelo.

Today the content is bounded by cultural deficiency in the so-called working classes, and the form kites above the clouds in modern art. The truth has no voice and the voice has no body: ends bleat.

Croesor for the foreigner is where the broom lives to sweep his false commitments away; the broom is the wind, uninterrupted in its passage by the coffin of progress—Industrialism—from which Lazarus alone can rise: his only cradle.

In being reduced to one's own absurdity may one not mount on to one's proper elevation: the earth?

Here, in Croesor, there is *nothing* of formalized certainty. There is nothing, literally nothing, of this modern thought-world. The sheep shapes nothing out of one's heavy gaze; he carves the hole in one's eye. The Cnicht is bald and alone; and proves Nature's creative concern by his absence of the sentimental kind. There is nothing; that means, there is room for anything; and when that anything, born here, finds the bleak and vast *palais de danse* too unbounded, its conceiver must move on, for the more spectacularly abrasive contexts of other, more inhabited, places. One must always lose most of the potential in order to achieve the minimum of the actual; the world is a fair distillery, because time retorts.

So:

'. . . the stuff of art endures as long as man. The fountain dwindles away only when men are rent and wasted by a sterile conflict, and the pulsing movement of society is halted. All this movement is creative because it is not a simple oscillation but a development unfolded by its very restlessness. The eternal simplicities generate the enrichment of art from their own bosoms not only because they are eternal but also because change is the condition of their existence. Thus art is one of the conditions of man's realization of himself, and in its turn is one of the realities of man.'[1]

---

[1] *Illusion and Reality*, Christopher Caudwell (Macmillan, 1937).

PART THREE

Living in Croesor

PAGES FROM A WINTER JOURNAL

Pages from a Winter Journal

December 1960–April 1961

December 14th 1960

Mrs. Williams is to close her shop after Christmas, for ever.[1] During the last months her shelves have been bleak. Two lonely bottles of 'Uncle's Sauce' (how wise not to be Uncle) are on the left. On the right: butter and lard; cream crackers; some tobacco; sad cleaning things below. The trouble is that so many villagers have cars, or can be given lifts, and do their shopping in the town. Speaking as a public institution. Mrs. Williams has long complained that few will 'support me'. A pity, Her shop is the source of priceless information. Its closing down is, to Croesor, like that of the *News Chronicle* to the larger community.

There are even rumours of Mrs. Jones closing the post office.[2] Mrs. Jones, from whom I borrowed in some kind of an association *East Lynne* and the Duchess of Windsor's memoirs, and I don't much converse. We deal with the weather in sometimes the vibrant tones of committedness. She is a person of extraordinary fundamentalism of character. Absolutely four-square upon her piece of ground, undeviating, apparently shock-proof, organic; as incapable of falsity as of flying to the moon. She is thus old-fashioned, and regrets even the overhead electricity wires. With much sifting, life still has the characteristics of a sequence of personally meaningful events to her. The adventitious is known but ignored; and she does not experiment with opinions. Her eyes, a little cramped by modern surrounds, over-curtained but sharp in those frames, are windows into a gone world, when living was not a doubtful occupation. The handrails providing her sense of security are invisible in the mists of time; her grasp of them

[1] A Welsh eternity; it is reopened in conjunction with the Post Office (1962).
[2] She has done so (1962).

153

is psychic. So secure is she as to look 'natural'; she is not dishevelled with the panic to know what will appear to be interesting in the cause of her 'personality'. So her rhythm is even and her atmosphere peaceful; but she is as alert in its defence—the defence of an ideology—as her dog Monty, who is now mine. Being well fitted into her context of memory, she acquires great significance; she lacks the contemporary fidgets. Those who refuse to 'move with the times' mark, by their static strength and their subterranean life, both the superficial and the actual passing of those times by their doors; progress looks like the rage of its petticoats through her eyes. One fancies the potential—one doesn't know how mentationally actual in flitting nuances of imminent perception—insight of such people to be vast. Gorki, in *Through Russia*, brought unsurpassed articulacy to such people. What interests me is that the image one receives of their *potential* meaning is nearer to that of my favoured artists, my 'great men' (by which I mean men straightforward to the extent of genius), than the clickety-needle-minded sprinters after contemporaneity. The Noble Savage and the Simple Person have been kennelled in cliché because clever people have never come to terms with their embarrassing realities. Even the bones of uncritically accepted opinion that such simple people hold firm between their untiring jaws acquire some of the juices, by salivation provoked, of a greater meaning: a meaning of symbols. Conversely, enlightened opinion can be bone-dry when unappetitively (modishly) twirled in a cocktail mind.

N—— smacked the baby today (she does so very rarely). I, who have so much less to do with the b., feel a humbug when I remonstrate, in some luxury of enlightenment: it's the luxury I rightly suspect. Obviously I haven't quite learned the truth of what I merely believe. Or if I know it, my knowledge isn't integrated in my practice, but my practice is stuck on as an advertisement of something still cold-stored in the premises somewhere out of light of mind. Persistent laziness in refraining from thinking into consciousness morally accepted principles may, through inertia, lead to the losing of such principles; the man who died of being right. Was Léautaud not one of these? A charming man. But in order to see what a butler can, he eschewed getting out of the employee mind: by directionless protest he was doubly bound.

Writing once must have been whispering to God. Now I write this in Bryn, the house opposite and above Bryn Hyfryd. It belongs to a business man who kindly allows me to work here while he is away. Having no God makes no difference; the part of a potential reader whom one addresses is *exactly* the same. *Exactly*. If the reader knew how one worships that part . . . he would think less of the writer, no doubt, in this age of tin-godly experts. However, I worship it; it is like an eye of light. It may condone the ostentation and error of expression; I am not a 'self-' expresser, having done my best to write the 'self' away.

Monty is restless, and we shall walk down to Bryn Hyfryd to cook supper: tonight, hash, made of corned beef and boiled bacon surmised into a rare dish. One can't know what one does until one does something about it—e.g. writes it—*if* (like me) one has a terror of unconsciousness; writing is lighting. People who fear unconsciousness make bad citizens; they grumble to consciousness of identity, like Monty to canineness.

December 15th

Those with ears can hear the voices of writers in their writing. Since the sound of voices is partly conditioned by the shape of the mouth, those imagined voices can be given shapes in the roughest and most far-fetched relationship with the mouths—far-fetched to make reasonable critics shy, which is a worthy aim always. Noble persons write ovoidly; those associated with them, in Gothic arches. Demagogic plebs write in flat slippers; genuine workers have a song (not in their hearts). Royal persons may write with a refreshingly arbitrary distribution of emphasis, such as I came across in George VI's letters. Henry James wrote in triangles; Lord Attlee in very thin oblongs standing on end; D. H. Lawrence in rubber blocks, sometimes moist. Lord Morrison writes in tin-tacks; he's trying to keep the ceremonial red carpet down in a gale. Odd: T. E. Lawrence has a touch in his style of the arbitrary (original) distribution of emphasis and, more specifically, an original metre that I've ascribed to royal persons; that's why he's among the most refreshing writers to read. He lacks all slogan-blocks with which Profound writers drug us to unthinkingness.

The Duchess of Windsor writes with the usual lack of *continuative* intelligence that we expect of royal persons. Partly their not being allowed to offend, partly their being unable to offend to much point. But their individual items, words and phrases, are like isolated castles with some history within (history in attitudes); continuity-intelligence, there if the drawbridge had been down, is cut by the raised bridge. Some spectral irrelevance, much coaxing of sympathy. ('Continuity-intelligence', obviously, intelligence in development, as opposed to masks, monuments, exorcising appeals to magnificence, absolutes, rubbish of ceremony, etc.) The Duke of Windsor, for instance, has a style like those unopened packing-cases in Citizen Kane's mansion, at the end of that film. Through it runs rivers of clear air—space between uninspected premises; rather pleasing; the Duchess's style is more crammed without being dense, though denser than expected. Figurines on conveyor-belts of the uninspected 'times'. But she writes with character, which she possesses. (I have long, but not very innocently, wondered at the lack of 'psychological' studies of the effects of monarchy. When I was thirty-five I dreamed I had tea with George VI, and we both wore red socks: the one time I've been a bit bashed about was, within a few years of this dream, by a rival over a girl, and we were both wearing red socks. He claimed the red of his was better than that of mine.) My mother brought me up in the glow of two facts of my origins. (1) We were descended from a—not very, I discovered—noble Irish family and (2) from the last High King of Ireland. I think she was thinking here of the branch headed by the O'Conor Don, who spells his name with one 'n', and that she may therefore be wrong. The point is she infused into me before I reached the age of treason to her information the common English romanticism anent royalty and nobility; since this is embarrassing I have with relish thought much on it, because the most interesting ideas in England are usually the most embarrassing. Wilde also enjoyed or suffered from this aberration, and so did the Duke of Windsor.[1] The formalistic repression of Labourite

[1] i.e. It is to be expected that the Royal Family shares the popular attitude to itself.

demagogues to these atmospheric airs (licensed by Robert Burns' honest 'a man's a man for a' that' for treacherous exploitation) is part of their sprung coyness; by formal denial they collude with the denied. They are almost sexually inverted in the emotional chores consequent. (See them at—some time ago, in the days of Ernest Bevin—a Savoy Hotel Palais Glide.) Most forthright English being as good as is but a modern mode of forelock-touching; to state is to abort the implicit. On the credit side of the upper classes is, in some cases, a degree of sensory versatility, sensory culture—in a minority, however: Philistinism seems astonishingly more endemic. Lord David Cecil, for instance, lacks flairs of nuances such as we may find in Gorki or even in W. H. Davis. As for D. H. Lawrence . . . There is a hint, in a monarchy, that socially eminent people should do things better than their inferiors; a hint that royal persons should write better, more accepted in a slightly stronger hint that dons should write better; how often have ploughboys, by disturbing the hint, expelled out of mysticism the royal functions, and the not unrelated academic ones. Democracy has certain unwashable traits in the best of rational detergents—this is one of them. Yet urbanity, *belles-lettrism*, 'felicities' (of the Sunday literary journalist kind) all bespeak a royalist orientation. In retaliation men of great talent have often been reactively reduced to unnecessary plainness, and tried to concoct a virtue therefrom. There's none. Raymond Mortimer writes as off gold royal plate at a royal function; Lawrence, as at *fêtes-champêtres*. Much Puritanism both in character and in writing (Wingate, T. E. Lawrence) shows anti-royalist bearings; Edward Marsh, the virtues culled from the opposite. Both contribute. Philistinism is more today to be found in *belles-lettrism* than in Beat.

Upper-class public manners are good, so are working-class manners. Vulgarity is a prerogative of middle-class refinement, grossened into pseudo-forthrightness and honesty in the rising meritocracy. The conflict between Soviet emissaries and social democrats is quite analogous to that between the middle and the aristocratic classes inland; the Soviets being imbued with the aristocratic trait of unequivocalness. Nietzsche in philosophy, D. H. Lawrence in writing, are the authorities in all this. Good manners consist in unaggression, bad manners in the padding of brutality. The English still respect aggression, confusing it with honesty; is this because they have always despised its restrictions in their major talent, commerce? Probably.

Finally aesthetics of living will become of supreme importance. The English literary middle class may be dead; but their cemeteries are crowded with flowers, mostly wax.

Security produces good manners (upper class); but when it's the security of a minority, a core of offensiveness is never absent. Working classes have also a kind of security; their manners are in constant growth, and the curse of them is in the frontier where they meet the middle-class ones. Anyone who has seen working-class delicacy has seen a human aristocracy therein. They are almost as good as animals (in speed of reflex—the soul of manners, inhibition being the vulgar body).

The Duchess's book is crowded with characters who lack character, being class stereotypes, but more vibrant being American, where the conventional retains some *brio*. It much resembles the half-dozen or so books of memoirs by society hostesses which I make a point of enjoyably reading. They retain an experimentally gastronomic attitude to human behaviour; they '*deguste*' one another, and have a fine range of condiments—in a crowded and unventilated restaurant. Whereas social whores have dingily narrow standards in behaviour, having no functional premises. Labour respectability (which disintegrates in Labour bohemianism—never separate these two) is commodity-motivated. Physical whores are society's most respectable class, and social democrats, for the same reason, the next most respectable. In the case of the former (physical) it's the source of their pathos and poetry being so anomalous. In the latter it's the source of their prose which is unending.

Night of December 15th

Having nearly finished the Duchess's memoirs—which are written in a style of great literary deportment (the phrases and clauses being martialled in orders of precedence like that of a court *levée*, so that you can catch mousy whispers of complaint here and there)—I'm again brought to consider the sensory experimentation (which is progressive) of this social class. It was what attracted Wilde and so many others to them, and constitutes their social glamour, for which middle-class morality has never been a successful alternative. This is of course distinct from intelligence, but not from its groundwork, its soil. In contrast revolutionaries are stereotypical in the same field; they are the most economical digits to which humanity can be reduced, stripped for the fight, therefore the most conventional of their times, therefore ethically and sensorily backward. Hence Puritan and authoritarian overtones and hangovers in all revolutions. Engineers are not yet artists. Man's progress is towards diversified appetites, the cultivation of which has always been decadent and immoral according to prevailing mores. The contribution of decadents is to manners and sensory enlargement of experience, towards therefore integration of mind and matter: basis of civilization: 'sophistication into eternity'. It is the path of diminishing surprise, diminishing action, re-absorption into that from which we came. De Sade a pioneer, and Edward Lear otherwise, invertedly. (Humour.) To believe in luxury (as opposed to pigging it) is a sign of a first-rate intelligence. When the nerves sing the brain dances: holy. I am pleased to see the great increase in the appreciation in England of good food and wine: Cyril Ray, etc.

Dichotomy: the opposite (by resemblance) of a dialectical relationship. We have today a great sense of dichotomy, because little or none of dialectic; which makes us romantically misanthropic. We dramatically, or rather melodramatically, like to see—indulge our own status in seeing—senselessly opposed thoughts, reasons, customs, to nourish our pretty despair. Consider the 'obscenity' arguments: (a) the publication of obscenity liberates a large part of human consciousness, and by so doing is creative; (b) the publication of obscenity by its sensationalism aborts what it attempts to prosecute—civilized acceptance of 'all sides of life'. With regard to (a), we find traces here of belief in absolute values, an unwillingness to note the prolific offshoots of repression, its 'dark' flowers (Baudelaire's 'of evil'). When, in defiance of the obvious creations arising from repression ('decadent'), we opt for 'frankness', we get the new Puritanism of D. H. Lawrence;

his use of 'obscenity' robbed obscenity of its positive function, the sexualism it covers in its shocking form. The colloquialism for the word copulate, for instance, is, used by the working class, a defence of a pleasurable activity by the use of a private, idiomatic term; and yet the cultural progress that demands that a private, only quasi-acceptable, activity should be brought into that part of consciousness furnished with concepts attaching to such words as copulate, let alone 'love', demands thereby a natural use of the word copulate or love—not as polite camouflaging, but springing from a mature and cultured and civilized acceptance of an activity only inhibitedly accepted in the terms of its colloquial equivalent. So the public, cultured acceptance of the colloquialism (implemented by the acceptance of the printed colloquialism) is the last and subtlest agent of the prevention of the cultured acceptance of the activity it denotes; the word and the deed are again prophylactic against full acceptance of pleasure. Hence the Puritan thrill of 'emancipation' among all concerned. Once again the opposition is bought into the Establishment, and life lies stranded outside Parliament. Provoked, this, by a very intelligent defence and exposition of Henry Miller in an old *Horizon* by Lawrence Durrell. He recognizes Lawrence's Puritanism, but incorrectly fails to recognize Miller's even greater Puritanism: Miller will not cross the border into cultured consciousness, but heats his side of the line into the dimensions of a world which, because it is dichotomic, is phantastic. The result? The *élan* goes, the juice dries, the 'roaring chaos', etc., of Miller, wilts into anarchic suburbanism. Lawrence endures better: he got over the border—but 'it' died in the crossing—the Man Who Died.

The criterion of great art is normality—its sense of that, and our sense of it in reading it. All pressures are transitory; enduring art leaves, as the acid of an engraving leaves, shapes meaningful beyond polemical usages. That Miller may apart from this pressured and topical significance have something else is possible; but it will be in despite of his 'obscenity': the flaw being that he, Miller, thinks he is obscene. This is a great limitation. Obscenity is an entirely subjective and contemporary judgement, which is why it is unnecessary. It operates mainly in judgements made of writing as obscene (on the censoring side) but secondarily in writing that courts such judgements: in other words, we have a dichotomy. The obscene delusion in sex is created by the publicization of inhibitedly secret satisfactions; a victim of the parent dichotomy of 'public' and 'private', which social change, not courageous 'frankness', will slowly anneal. Of course, given the astringent meanness of censorship, that overt Puritanism, one may allow the uses of obscenity, that invert Puritanism. The whole matter is so irrelevant that it becomes a major red herring, constitutes a delusional criterion of emancipation. I don't know; I know I wouldn't bother. Storms in teacups distract one from storms at sea. It is analogous to attacking religion instead of one of religion's functions—exploitation to preserve its other function—towards communion. If opium becomes the religion of the people, sex becomes the religion of opium eaters.

But where, now, is the Duchess?

Durrell's article has an excellent quotation from Proust, which I'll reproduce as an armament against critics:

> 'A well-read man will at once begin to yawn with boredom when anyone speaks to him of a new "good book", because he imagines a sort of composite of all the good books that he has read and knows already, whereas a good book is something special, something incalculable, and is not made up of the sum of all previous masterpieces, but of something which the most thorough assimilation of every one of them would not enable him to discover. . . .'

True, except that the prejudiced incomprehension of critics of a new masterpiece dialectically serves, by providing animately the criteria, the inclusion of the new masterpiece in the critical canon. Without intelligent opposition, no positive acceptance later. Even stupid opposition illuminates (more than the dull features of the critic). Then, great critics will say: 'What has this to do with Croesor?' I will reply: 'What have I to do with great critics?' And will hear a voice saying: 'As much as this has to do with Croesor.' And will answer the voice: 'Plenty.' Limitation of fields—'specialization'—is the agent of confusion. Eventually, just as one 'authentic, ineffable, autonomous individual' has nothing to do with another ditto, one blade of grass

L

will also be severed from the community of grasses, and we'll go up when the Bomb comes down, grass and all: aerially 'authentic, ineffable, autonomous individuals'. Atomization is social as well as physical; the two categories converge in war (next). Durrell commends Miller's alleged formlessness, seeing in it a sign of constant growth, superabundant energy, creativity, etc.; enlisting Lawrence in support, another 'extra-literary' writer. Possibly; yet much of formlessness is the finding of a new yet spurious content through destruction of forms that would otherwise be obsessive—this, inevitable among the better writers in an age of contracting formalism. There again we have a dichotomy. Form and formlessness are not creative opposites: everything perpetrated, marked down, is a shape; every shape is a good or bad form. Usually formlessness means just bad economy; because there is an economy of form in its expressive power of content inherent in any work of art. 'Formlessness' at the lowest level means the nihilistic bruhaha of a neo-creative talent; like contentlessness, the opposite, in which 'polished' form is everything. Formlessness may mean an equal self-consciousness *about* form. Neither form nor formlessness as such are criteria of good writing; always a specific form in relation to its specific content. Whitman, and Lawrence's verse (as he well knew and said), are very formal in relation to their content; Lawrence's free verse is strictly economized to the needs of his content. In degree of the lack of this organic economy (form as the economically determined vehicle of content), so the extraneous form—formalism—becomes inevitably (necessarily) a new, inarticulated content on its own account, like the germination through disintegration of all organic matter. The last, I think, form of optimum brilliance still economically wedded to content is in Henry James. His content has never been developed therefrom; his form, of course, influenced too many. But in James content, like a leaking cloud, sullies here and there the sky of form. They are, according to the rules, integumented with each other; a mixture of passenger and vehicle, but still travelling. But of course form is but the medium of comprehensibility for (today) an absconded public. It is free—to be 'creatively inarticulate', anarchically breeding its own pseudo-peripheral content.

Free form will always *tend* to mean unresolved content; but the latter may be justified as experiment: new—really new—content may, and may not, necessitate new form: whether or not is historically determined, according to the health, the dynamic uses of accepted form. Today, when everything is known about good writing and the good book, good writing and the good book don't appear (apart from the critics' weekly discoveries of masterpieces, which is also what I mean). The author is frustrated by what he knows the critic demands he should write. That is, above all, what he should not write. Critics may be right appreciators and useful (always inaccurate) exegetes; but they are harmful as vicarious creators (e.g. Pritchett).[1] It is the very *art* of criticism (cf. Wilde) that prevents the latter catastrophe, distinguishes criticism properly from creation vicariously of the work being considered.

Critics should also have a profound historical (socio- and cultural) sense; it is their awful impressionism ('I *feel* . . .') that makes them such scalliwag tarts. They become sensuously impressionable tarts, slithering forward to positions of maximum susceptibility, and dropping their brains *en route*. A critic waits to be raped by a masterpiece, instead of caring to understand; if the masterpiece doesn't rape him, he sues for breach of promise and rags it. Books get to know this and adorn themselves with the aggressive tokens of 'genius'—hence, one masterpiece a week.

December 16th

Since men don't feel responsible rulers of themselves (but swung from the teats of mystic matriarchs) they punish cruelly attempts at responsibility, which take increasingly criminal forms; the moral hordes of *East Lynne*. One punishes on principles inorganically ingested; never on one's own reflection. Only principles of another, uncomprehended by oneself, can serve as weapons of offence. The more irritatingly inorganic these principles are, the more furiously do they become weapons of aggression. That is what we mean by the horde: and the horde is always ruled by one of themselves: no one else

---

[1] But Schnabel (*My Life and Music*) explains that writers write for the public, not for the artist.

could bear to do it. The horde is coagulated child-man, undifferentiated, and differentiated therefore by pseudo-individuality. Caliban's rulers must be as ugly as Caliban in order that he shall feel his own beauty. There is, alas, the most indirect justice in this. Hence the greatest punishers, violent righters of wrong, always feel the voice of God running through them; they can complacently fail to understand this voice (its *raison d'être*), and obey it violently, with nice little conscience (pep) kicks throughout. Civilized judges who progressively abdicate from the bench listen to Jesus or reason. A judge is a weapon of the past.

If people lack the desire to be violent, laws against violence will provoke them to it, and punishment return them to their mother's arms.

Punishment suppresses people into a false, phantastic community of infancy; with their brains in the separated executive. Forgiveness is the subtlest assumption of punitive powers. It drives the simple mad.

A paper in Birmingham asks (reviewing my *L.V.*) if any writer of worth has ever written intimately about himself. 'Good taste' is involved, i.e. it would be bad taste to taste intimately in public a particularly succulent dish of beef, would it not? Andreyev somewhere says of people that they still bathe in frock-coats . . . or the image is used. Quite. This noxious and sickening separation of public and private . . . comes, of course, from an ingrained sense of personal dirt, deriving I suppose from commercial schemes and Puritan sex. Infantilism run mad. Space, dear sir, forgives *you*; Time will take longer about it.

Another reviewer, to instance how badly I write, describes my style as a mixture of Pound and J.-J. Rousseau. I'm an ardent admirer of Rousseau—a man I love—and others admire Pound. Strange world.

A final word on accusations of egotism against those who write about themselves. The chronic or dedicated or worthwhile autobiographer is the man who has left himself sufficiently to have been forced to give adequate shape to his self-conception; exiled, he rebuilds conceptually. Hence, he is the least of egotists, being a stranger to himself; he to himself is as others are to him: strangers to become known. Many other aspects too . . . should one reply to fools? No. One should learn from them the way of the world.

It would be good taste not to taste intimately in public a particularly succulent dish of beef, would it not? Love apart and fight together: your dear community. It is good taste not to taste. It is polite to die.

However: the process is—public manners to educate individuals. Inevitably—it is so. The public minuet. The process: individual contributions to publicized codes; public codes then repressively but also educatively used on private individuals—by that time, out of date to many. It's so. Can't be helped. Not to side with one or another part of a process. Pax. Anarchy is as stupid as authoritarianism; they're husband and wife and come to sense in their endless arguments ('no doubt').

See in Croesor, where public and private are so near, so that the agent of their (principled!!) separation is a nervous tic, and gossip that of their propinquity. Croesor prepares for Christmas. There's a party at the school this afternoon; Bob Owen gives the presents every year to the children. Nellie's going; we're not because the baby isn't well. The *Liverpool Daily Post* from an interview says I'm a character; never. I am not lovable enough for drowning in the soft bosom of the public; besides, I don't understand their game at all. Such an entanglement of *entendus,* such a wealth of semi-forthrightnesses. O English forthrightness—as clear as the Sphinx. Consistency is probably a good road to contemporary fame; that this means stereotype is sufficient criticism. Always being the same, eventually when you're alone. But every day is for a new self; only the posthumous is recognizable. Forgetting what you said is a hygienic discharge; no room for more otherwise. No guarantee that you're not remembering, as opposed to thinking (the difference isn't as obvious to all as it should be). Motto: always write what you don't know (I see Auden agrees): because to write what you do know (textbooks apart) separates writing from meaning, both being integrated in the actual writing/thinking process; thus making writing descriptive, which is deadly.

I write to discover what I think; clarity can, and usually does, hide the muddiest of premises; obscurity is often an adherence to clear premises at the risk of compromising clarity. There is often a point at which clarity becomes inimical to integrity, because the language by long usage holds the concepts of the Opposition; new ideas inevitably compel new meanings of words (one of the advantages, by the way, of autodidacticism). When such a point occurs, I had rather stick to my guns obscurely than earn an order of merit by employing a falsifying clarity. I admire clarity and strive for it; but it must be organically and integrally *achieved*—not anticipated.

Order is the crown of revolution, I mean.

I once wanted to be an active person: I was a gang-leader in childhood, and wanted to continue later; most of my passivity is inversion of that past desire, fear- or shock-induced. As an active person I would have been openly 'offended', 'stood up for my rights', and tried to secure a *social* position and existence. Therefore, when I read military memoirs of a certain kind (which I enjoy terribly), I tremble and do become 'offended', etc.; I've just read Sykes's excellent *Orde Wingate*. This hero—Wingate—is the latest example of a kind that has always fascinated me (in fiction, Conrad): T. E. Lawrence, Livingstone, Schweitzer, Gandhi, Lenin, to an extent Winston Churchill: the kind of men who managed (or were conditioned) to fit their undoubted individualistic genius into some degree of orthodox success and recognition—outsiders who got in, not to be confused with Labourites who go Right. There's a kind of balance there; I think eternal outsiderism tends to a neurotic condition, unless absolutely essential according to contemporary circumstances—circumstances in which an orthodoxy can dispense with genius, or has no need of it. Wingate satisfies completely this admiration. The great soldier's belief in God is feasible, if not reasonable; without that, his intelligence would turn him against his profession. However, outsiderism is today sufficient of a cult to be a prestige name for its opposite, orthodoxy—new recruits, a new hired opposition.

That greatness or genius can support an orthodoxy is of some interest. (Marx never denied it, but certain faithful communists appear to want to do so.) Such men are deep, vintage individuals, so long ago laid down as to have become potent enough to marry (through their particular 'faiths', and even without faith) political reaction with their inherent skills. They take their work in the manner of artists in the restricted sense—art for its own sake, whether they're soldiers or whatever. Scientists appear sometimes to have been thus. Quite clearly, and for obvious reasons, orthodoxy can contain a diminishing number of such men. But the great skirmisher was Brecht, who adopted a Schweik technique.

Three orthodox and enjoyable biographies recently: Wingate, Peter Green's *Kenneth Graham*, and Edward Marsh. All very good, all very English in their virtues (for the English are marvellous in writing of what they admire; never too eulogistic, their love of something (virtue in action, perhaps—perhaps just of the isolated human being) inspiring their careful, so well-built memorials). Literary men get worse biographies, and poets the worst. I have not read a good life of D. H. Lawrence, Rimbaud, Dostoevsky, Gorki, etc. Why? Because the biographer rarely understands both the life *and* the work. The connection hides its formula; Freud is of no—or little—help; Marxism is usually done with a trowel. Rimbaud has been horribly treated, by both the mystifiers and the moralists. Lawrence's place (despite the enormous amount of work on him) remains uncharted; because his working-classness is over- or underestimated in importance, and the *kind* of importance. It is not yet recognized that the sensibility of working-class people is *new*: not descriptively to be expressed, but as quite new. Most, of course, suppress its novelties in the process of becoming sufficiently cultured to write. Lawrence didn't. *Only* working-class sensibility has the quick connection between thought and action; its senses are next to its brain, and its heart in no wise disarmed. The rest—well, the major use of culture has been to build a platform from which to sound depths, creating those depths by social elevation away from them. This has value in a kind of objectification ... but in dead terms so often. Genius never leaves the earth for long; academies exist on space-platforms.

The world was entire when I played with my working-class friends in childhood; it then became divided into spirit and matter. Which is why artificial stimulants are taken—to animate matter and to materialize spirit. Drunkenness increases (with drugs) as the culture declines —which is when an impossible segregation of spirit and matter is achieved precisely *when* the (competitive) dynamic of their (bourgeois) separation is dying or dead. John Clare may have gone mad because his smatterings of culture were, like a kite, rising from his working-class sensibility; what in the rulers is sophistication is in the lower orders schizophrenia. Given an immense tension to integration, division is fatal. Only the honest go mad. There are some honest sane people; but their sanity has usually detracted from their insight, *à la mode*. (Wilhelm Reich recognized the integrity of the insane, and wrote very wonderfully about it.)

December 28th

Mrs. X was not invited to the Christmas party. Little plants, water press through the ground, moss covers the slate, the river flows and the sun shines but the dingy-mingy ploys of people, like stale washing, flap on: the flags of their frustration. Village morality and feuding (they're not quite distinguishable) are like the struggles of mad mice underground; as those of politicians are like those of larger rodents (disguised as lions of Judah) above ground. The small and large patterns are identical. In spite of this the community feeling I sensed on arrival prevails; much of it, I observe, through lack of those amenities of civilization that would help to break it up into more advanced individualistic warfare. Why presume to judge? When one realizes thoroughly that one has— thank heaven—no executive powers, one may cease to judge people; cease, that is, to indulge in rhetoric; democratic rhetoric is the language of slaves reciting odes to Freedom.

Problem: how to refrain from judging the judges. Solution: describe them.

Mrs. Jones says the sacredness has gone out of Christmas. She is probably the only one to regret it here. Most emancipation from such matters—'holy Christmas'—takes the form of drunkenness in Oxford Street. Progress? Ha ha. The loss of a crutch is no guarantee of being able to walk. I gave Mrs. Jones V. Gollancz's religious anthology. I like Gollancz; he bothers still to act upon his beliefs. He reminds me of a spiritual Kerouac, whose *Dharma Bums* is a nice book, very gentle if not very profound. The underground unconscious symbolist opposition is very complex, very difficult to unravel. Peter Green's *Kenneth Graham* is very good; like Kerouac, another man essentially of peace, astutely without the *conscious* intelligence to be compromised into rebellion. How many more orthodox outsiders? Surely, though, we'd better call outsiderism a Tory phenomenon? Not quite. Kerouac's 'rebellion' is like that of a singing dog serenading the master's castle. His voice is really soft enough to be allowed in; his only embarrassment, his sense of music. But Tennyson managed it. Kerouac is like Tennyson. Ginsberg, I think, has never been outside the castle; will he be kicked out? His talent seems to deserve it.

Study of a literary friend; a youngish man old in the vintage manner of a *littérateur*, a failure. Swathed in ancient literary ardour as ever; his wild eye looks through the literary ardour most wildly, despairing now of ever being confirmed in what he suspects he is by being significantly contradicted in his fishing lies about himself. He lies, hoping emotionally, but not factually, to be found out. I found him out long ago; but to contradict him would be to confirm the lie, not what 'he is', which anyway is too much devoured by what he says. A hangover of the emotional opera of twenties and thirties: belief in the divinity of strong feeling, ragged with the racket of intoxicating sincerity: sincerity is already available as Pep Pills. He still stews himself into authentic states of being—a kind of auto-hypnosis into significance. The trouble is, this significance thus achieved is inapplicable in works. When he works he feels insignificant, because his spontaneous discoveries upset the premises upon which his significance rests. An unhappy man: his fatality, to silence what he wants to hear from others about his suspected condition; when he succeeds, he wears a questioning expression: so he's not aware of his silencing technique, which is perfected. Trouble is, he wants just a little of the truth about himself so that it may condimentally spice the lie into plausibility. Like a hovercraft, his levitation and his speed make his superficiality feel 'creative'. This is not pleasantly written, because animus takes refuge in keeping sealed the concept 'lie'—deplorably inexact. A more functional view of people dispenses with a moralistic judgement of this kind, which comes from a static attitude. But the wish not to harm people cannot (by me anyway) be morally achieved. Until I *see* the, as it were, lively inaccuracy of so doing, I shall persist. Always a moral principle is conducive to the practice of what it condemns, because the form of a principle prevents the perception of its scientific or functional correctness. So Christianity remains an enemy of socialism.

People's deficiencies (so-called) are impromptu strategies of survival, strictly geared to their environments; their 'deficiency' is purely lack of understanding, over which collectively society could exercise control, but over which individuals can have none whatsoever. At most, they may learn from others—without much conviction, since on a basis of what must basically remain faith. Only a dynamic social system merits the individual respect accorded to necessity, which the individual's shared dynamicism converts into freedom by understanding.

To say The End is fatuous; T. S. Eliot's (his period's) limited intelligence is inherent when he says 'in our end is our beginning': the end is too arbitrary even to contain a beginning: we have a rhythmical continuation, in which certain abrupt conclusions delude us into ends and beginnings: each of which merely reflects failure in concentration. End/beginning is a unit of inspiration which, broadened, makes continuity.

Mistinguette is worth reading; all simple (or foolish) people contribute more by diffusion in reflection of their times than all but the genius contribute by synthesis. Avoid philosophers and read fools, with exceptions.

December 29th

A drink with Michael Young, who looks tired. He admitted that at one time he hadn't been averse to having power; not averse to having a great deal, I thought. (He once said he couldn't enter Parliament because he couldn't be sure of maintaining his integrity. This was far-sighted, and if applied would considerably deplete the House.)

He has more (conventional) virtue than anyone I've met of his intellectual status. In ten years, seeing him on and off, I have never got to know him. His *Meritocracy* is good but suffers from the fault, common to satires, of here and there embalming into inapplication certain truths obviously not satirically intended. This makes the satirical intent an evasion of principles and perceptions that he fails to implicate. He (who is very educated) regards education as remote in its effects from talent or genius; he also once told me that law had nothing to do with ethics, a piece of information that I have guarded and prized. It is beautifully true. Has more the manner than the silly matter of modesty; esteems personal matters above impersonal or public ones, and has a remarkably impersonal manner of speaking, and a remarkable lack of personal animus against anyone. A student *par excellence*. He looks deeply nostalgic, like so many of us of around his age: a generation ruptured from family into publicity without graduation. Hence their silly, continued, 'dramatic' contrast, their schizophrenic effects; and pessimism. In speaking he thinks on the spot: a rare courtesy in these pre-thinking days.

Peace is still here; I walked into my 'church' today, which is any unpopulated piece of country. Heaving mountains like hearts up into the mists of thought. Birds and sheep. The nonsense in oneself walks quietly out of the premises; yet a time comes, sometimes, when one's grinning mask, replete with grinning phrases, stares down at one from an accommodating configuration of rock. I know this well. A lovely place; looking down, I see Nellie on the way to a bonfire with rubbish, children in our 'high street'.

December 30th

Re Wilson's *Finland Station*: an old-fashioned man; he believes, in spite of a rich historical sense, in man's 'will'; he opts for 'I decided', as though a new world was instantly born. Decision is a sensation, and 'I' is a related sensation of separation—arbitrary, functional, generic, unreal individually. 'I decided': two compendia of unknown processes, blocked and packed into idols of the moment, to serve the ideology of individual freedom, man's up-to-the-minute folly. The opposite is not fatalism; it is community planning and direction. Individualistic freedom is, *au fond*, fatalistic, being a sensation stealing from an opposite fact. 'Decided': pleasurable release of tension confused with following effects, attached sentimentally; a magic by mimesis. Look: that 'I' (and I think the world is assumed to inform this 'I') alleged to have exploded magically new configurations of reality. New —as though I created them. Thus, as though I created 'I'. But actually? I, to that small chronic degree the self-observer, watched 'me' (subject-pronoun of the verb), the actually impelled clothes-horse of actional dress, sliding into certain actions; a fortuitous assembly. *I will* is pure magic, pure sensation emulating actuality. The most heady, the most popular, the most ideological, sensation; the sensation allowing us to be controlled by other lunatics similarly dowered.

In London the cerebration ignited by passing crowds manages the perpetuity of this sensation. But the country returns one's awareness of environment; intimations of a creative link, only manifest in social control. Will is always envisaged as resistance; it may be true only in co-operation, by recognizing the necessary. Will in popular concept is least of all will; it is inflated futility in a mystique of divinity. A history of the 'I' concept (available from styles in literature and art) would show the contemporary peculiarities of the concept, its increasing modifications. I can only be born in them again. Its myth of isolation is dead. The metaphor, Christian baptism, has its future reality in socialism. The latter was a prophecy.

A madman can say: 'I am you.' One day this will be within the powers of the sane.

I: the wizard of metaphorical para-existence, the creator by mimesis of hallucinations of effects. Much of the history of 'I' is to be traced in the changing grammatical emphasis of the simple sentence; now we're adjectivally and adverbially overcrowded. The poor verb is nearly atomized, because the 'I's' impotence is becoming manifest—still tethered to his donkey, the verb.

I as collusion between subject and object: we could call it creatively fissionable for epochal functions.

My 'I' in London is like a comb whose teeth tingle as the hair of the sirens of proffered personality pass through them. But in Croesor it is the hair of a feather with others on a core. More adheres to it here, so more may be jettisoned. In London 'I' is a ball served by the tennis rackets of millions; so often roving the air as to cease to be associated with me. Here it may rest, nuzzle up to me; we converse and connect and refine to the merest nothing of obtrusiveness to perception. Our drama—horny and corny—is still the silly business of I contra the world, which is man fighting his reflection. I-world is a fact; like all facts, limited to the static experience *per se*. Solipsism is a deliriously extremist mode of self-education: making the world one's house to get out of that delusion when the last doorknob has been fixed. The ego cannot, for its own survival, oppose the world; it loves it, for its own survival. But it hates the presented bill from the world; fills its moat hurriedly when it sees the awful creditor coming. Delves, then, into fanfares of the mystery of self, from Freud's gasometer for this inflation. Techniques of the sexual love-match are the major education in one's dialectical relationship with the world: once learned in that purpose, love will desert sex, being no longer of this educational purpose. Sex will then increase into a *social* engagement (Huxley, in *Brave New World*, like much else in that alleged satire, unconsciously prophesies good things). The privacy of sex is therapeutic, and will one day be unnecessary: pornography, orgies, immorality, nude shows, are all educations to public sex—crudely, of course, educations to its proper socialization. The black sheep provides this wool. Sadistic sex is the neurotic experimentation towards social sex: a neurosis instigated by an uncomprehended perception of the call of vast spaces from the hermetic confines of sex love. On the other plane, asceticism is in the same experiment. The 'libel' on early Soviet sex practices (whence in bourgeois rectitude the Soviets have withdrawn) was an intuition of the inevitable—as always, appearing as anathema. That which should be, and isn't, is always cursed, when it's advanced to the extent of being under the skin. It makes the valiantly contemporary scratch painfully.

What's the contemporary definition of 'I'? Entirely negative: I = not you: as near a lie as can be. Only the I indistinguishable from the you will last; then individuality can grow flowers instead of thorns, laugh instead of snarling (Nietzsche's superman).

Private consumption makes the rheumatism of the private 'I', a sociological invalid at death's door; see Kafka.

But the public 'I', anticipating by parody, is emptier.

I rest in an 'I' denuded of social status, competitive afflatus, religion, nearly all mysticism; grossly undernourished through dislike of available nourishment; my I is the mere, unavoidable nexus of my observable operations, their alleged source. It is all that remains, and will die into you. You are immortal, one may say.

The abiding problem has been the search for a functioning I; Tolstoy, who wrote poems around the construct to achieve an ultimately viable distillation; Gorki, who retained a sort of anima, impersonal upon which new selves in better times could be grafted; Rimbaud, its explosion; Marx, of a race whose 'I' had always been conspiratorially intact, aided by a compelledly ruthless association of 'I' and survival, has an 'I' rising like a lion of wrath after millennia of captivity (the Jewish 'I' being the object of envious anti-Semitism). Nietzsche's 'I': the greatest opera of this concept; and the Taoist 'I'? The cow upon which the gentle man travelled. The union of Tao and Brecht is epochal. It is modern.

The 'I's in Croesor are primitive clouds, brushing against each other for just a little lightning now and then; their assertions are tentative, therefore graceful. Of such will be the kingdom of heaven on earth. But: all the 'I's that ever have been will concourse to the new river of 'I's; by discharging the local, be absolved into the general.

January 2nd/3rd 1961

We 'saw in' the new year with Edith and Michael. N—— laughed at Michael's air of discovery that the year read the same upside-down: her eyes are very quick, and save her immense 'thought'. According to Welsh custom (it seems) the children came round to collect money— but not on Sunday, because Chapel doesn't like money business on that day: we live by sin? The local belief is that it's unlucky not to give the children money. It might well be. Finished Wilson's *Finland Station*. The usual comic idea that our ideology isn't one but just grew and is 'natural', whereas the Marxian is one and is artificial. He calls the dialectic of Marx a rationalization. He makes no analysis of our ideology. Michael obviously right when he says the romantic appeal of communism has gone with the immense increase of the movement's strength; but the attractions of efficiency (when the complete decline of the gentleman's mystique of the superiority of inefficiency has come—it must soon) may be even greater in England. Attitudes to conditioning of mankind responsible for intellectual nebulosity; conditioning is pragmatically accepted, religiously minimized: in penology therapy displaces punishment through enforced acceptance of conditioning factors, while moralists rave and cry for the birch, etc. How can a society flourish when its central philosophy is inimical to scientific practice? When individual self-responsibility, the myth, is allowed to sabotage efficiency that is only possible in co-operation? Perhaps one should write to the *Daily Express* to find out. The feeling of control is in an inverse ratio to the fact of control! A general law of facts and feelings.

January 6th

The *opéra bouffe* of Personality at work: *TV*. An interviewer with the expression of a customs officer confronts the interviewed. The interviewer looks psychologically tightly packed, not a garment showing; the interviewed like a suitcase less well packed, with a pair of pants showing under the lid. The interviewer, we can see, is determined to have all the underclothes out. The fallacy: that the contents of the interviewed suitcase are vitally different from those of the interviewer. It could be a bullfight. Men as private, patentedly different enterprises; breeding the kind of curiosity that makes little boys lift little girls' skirts, and from the same reasons: of artificial segregation and resultant mystification. 'Cultural' employment depends increasingly on this myth of difference; how unutterably boring and banal it becomes. Our hope lies in what is common to us all. Life is in part the discovery of this commonness; we're brought up to expect the opposite. American 'news' (!!) magazines have reached heights of vulgarity in the 'personalization' of events—'history'!!!— that we cannot yet afford. Like a mad pawnbroker of souls, the President waggles witch-doctor eyes, making mystic payments on even more mystical pledges. Power! The waggler of wagglers smiles serene; *he knows he is being waggled*. Individuals will soon be attaching elephants' trunks and donkeys' ears to look even more inscrutable. They will soon be so inscrutable as to fail to recognize themselves. They will be inscrutable into insanity. I remember that comic movie called *The March of Time* when I was a child; no mere coincidence that this movie happened in the times of the dictators. I still remember the thrilledly 'awful' voice in which the presiding vocative nincompoop spoke of those dictators. Our individualism is in the inherited context. The movie was so funny that it died; its spirit moves on. The March of Time! O la.

In Croesor we're too near to be so different. None has the physical or psychic tic of a sense of uniqueness, or the hallucinated look (auto-hypnotic). Ben the farmer lacks all tics. My 'self-obsession' was an obsession with my not-self, the identity thrown at me, which stuck for certain reasons, but which I didn't digest. It was an obsession to get rid of that adhering not-self. Other people are the same; they are impaled on an 'ineffable' self which they know to be not true, which impedes their lives. They waste their lives in inner dialogues between what they are and what they are said to be. Partitions between people are paper-thin; therefore have to be all the more powerfully reinforced with the individuality cult. We work together and we drool apart. The 'I' is orphaned from a community imminently upon us. In cheap fiction the 'I' is tight as a bullet, shot through the story; a neurotic of the first water. Only arithmetically contrived plot can serve as his shooting gallery. If the plot be life, the 'I' is disintegrated.

January 7th

Christopher Wordsworth in the pub: what is his ploy? As a Tory outsider I suggested to him the high market value of his written-up personality. He will not, I think, relate himself to his survival, and so keeps the latter adventitious. This is rather profound, this unrelation; I don't blame him. It is rather a disgusting association, in the context. His *Underdogs* (Toynbee's symposium) is a very witty, very clever piece indeed, though curiously mannered: in the mannerisms, of course, lie C.'s soul. The mannerisms are those of un-self-supporting gentility, as above; having socially fallen out of the category, the category becomes incarnate in him. We have something in common, except that I fell out and down longer ago—in fact, am second-generation fall-out. He was trained as gentleman, I not. I know him very well —as a condition, I mean, not as a person. I also wouldn't lift a finger if it weren't for—for what? Pleasure, I think, in lifting it; I like the exercise. Besides, I've nothing to keep up—he has much to keep down, which is the same. He appears to me to have grown around his soul, like barnacles round a ship's bottom; it will soon be sealed up; will he then rise again? Probably. But his wit is excellent; a most undefeated man, though he flirts with defeat, as who wouldn't for the thrill and the graciousness of it, the utmost *politesse* of it in this striving and ambitious society? What more cordially yours than to fail? Dear brother? But he won't. He only flirts. I, when young, *blushed* if seen doing anything noticeably conducive to my survival. I think C. has the same 'pride'. But when, later, I 'indulged' in visible survival tactics, I went drunk with the luxuries of commonness—though always fearful of drowning therein—couldn't think, my thinking being irremediably linked to my old-fashioned individualism, which I curse.

Christopher is probably the most interesting person in the district: because he is a moving, forming one; what he does (kept to the minimum!) is related to what he is, and he likes the liberty of being this brings. A connoisseur of life, he knows the titbit by the wayside tastes better than the presented banquet; being eaten in the world. He is thoroughly self-employed, has the *drame portatif*. He may, one day, write a remarkable book; a last gentleman's-eye view of our pseudo-democratic marmalade, with rare insight into the rags of egalitarianism in which we serve our sentences. A little Stendhalian? Oh yes. A similar nose for democratic humbuggery hiding envy; a nose for class-gymnastics. Should observe the conflict of the co-operative 'soul' with the competitive mind. Could it be he has a starvation for community; can't bear the competitive exigencies? Won't he accept that what we have in common is fighting each other? Seems he won't; a poor citizen! His failing: too great a dedication to his personal drama; won't accept

M

that the theatre is a ruin, of this kind of thing. His achievement: wit. Re wit: the spirit laughs at what the heart has lost. So it should; the mind has gained it; brains alone being the feet of progress, which critics may unmix (the metaphor); 'when the mind forgives the body, it becomes it; and much intelligence is released'—Reich.

An example of 'acceptable' (as opposed to my) writing (*Evening Standard*): various specimens of marble 'were submitted to his scrutiny'. This is made possible because the scrutiny belonged to a high income group (Mr. Getty). Could one submit to a tramp's scrutiny? Mahogany-furniture English!—it's difficult to submit to a tramp's scrutiny.

January 13th

I was always unfortunately able to picture out of phenomena what I feared, and to see in human expressions some long-remembered angel or devil: such an explanation of projection would *seem* to 'account' for such 'hallucinations': not so: the projection of phantasy on to phenomena or people is not necessarily false perception: cf. Blake, and the golden thread through the lunatic eye. It may be just—I think it is—the perception of fact too vivid for the timorous consciousness to accept. Recalling people known in my over-impressionable (as they say—I'd say straight-seeing) youth, I find those whom I thought 'evil' were neurotic, dishevelled and anxious, for the peace of mind, to have their inner untidiness shared. All madmen look for converts, and are excruciatingly loving in so doing. I've known two or three.

To revert—to my unfortunate habit of seeing what I have been imagining—a proof of art?—I thought I saw the village moralist in the village today: yet, I may be wrong; yet, I may not be.[1] I tend to see what's below a person's rationalized social *persona*, indeed: am only now becoming aware of the equal importance of the *persona*. The latter is socio-historical, the former—genetical? Resistant, anyway, to the latter. But—the village moralist: wickedness to this lady (I judge all by what I saw—I don't know her at all) is snuff for a refreshing sneeze, clearing her nose of its bad smell of what she thinks is

[1] A visitor, I'm told.

humanity. She carries on trunk-like torso with care and significance the standard moral face, which is ubiquitous and as follows. The cheeks are creased round the nose and descend like sails from that mast of executive honour. The eyes are severely hemmed in by the constricting skin, which grudges all of that kind of space to them that would endanger critical perception by the inlet of imagination. The eyes, thus hemmed parsimoniously in, resemble a French ticket clerk suspiciously demanding through the *guichet* what one wants—probably evil. The eyes through this *guichet* are entirely assessing, and, in terms horribly, depressingly combined of economic and moral status—no distinction is allowed, and out of this the neurotic platform from which such conventional hallucinations are perpetrated is precariously constructed. They suffer from agoraphobic over-localization, and their owners pay God in coin of *this* realm as rent of their hutch. He smiles. They are self-appointed constables of the Lord, and are constantly cutting their wages to hide from themselves the pleasures of their office (masochism to justify sadism). They are empty, so they wag alien powers in their fearful grasp; and are vigilant in remembering what they think they think. The mouth is the two lines drawn above and below the addition of the unpleasant sum their policing eyes have assembled. Their words are parsimonious and issue in a tiny stream of colourless sibilants, punctuated here and there by granite tables of the law (particularly hard consonants, wearing the innuendoes of involuntariness).

This lady's wag of the head when I greeted her with suitable nervousness was like that of an haute-couture model's at a passing tramp; she smelled me with her clothes. She then returned to a profoundly blind contemplation of the landscape—I looked at what she was looking at and was satisfied that it was constructed of nothing more positive than not-me. In such a village as this, such people are unimportant; but at a national level they are murderous. Besides, Croesor has a man of large soul in opposition to such people—Bob Owen, who has spoken to me of his protests against, for instance, preachers who concentrate lustfully on the wickedness of mankind, who attack where they should encourage. It is quite remarkable how Bob has merrily remained outside the narrow orbit of such Welsh Puritanism;

it is one source of his unusual sophistication, not cynical, but comprehending of the greater world. Another great opponent lives nearby—John Cowper Powys.

I may have imagined this lady; but Blake has defined imagination to include such hallucinations; and hallucination is but the protective term the polite consciousness gives to straight sight. After all, we must not be murdered by what we see!

Mrs. Jones escapes all this. Her post office is a haven. She never changes; dumpy, cheerful, always kindly, leaning very far over the bar of her principles, she well knows that life exists also on the other side. Like Bob, she has an innocent eye. Both feel safe in the world; and this sense of total security (or security in the totality, if not in the locality) is the source of mental and spiritual adventure out of the ruts of non-thinking progression. Such people like themselves, which makes them the object of the sharpest envy; egalitarian tape-measures are produced —who does he think *he* is? The point is, he doesn't think of who he is. Only Topsys bypass the constricting standardizations of a world too primitive to afford true individuality. Those who just growed alone can answer those who couldn't just. Around such over-localization as the moral lady the mountains bound with unbinding beauty, and the river sings at the top of its voice; it's in flood today.

January 15th

A hard frost and sparkling sky last night, the river rasping refreshingly along its bed. Morning, a heavy white frost, no wind and sunshine: the silence of a theatre at curtain-rising. So the Actors appear, infallibly. Strong men with guns and hounds arrive to kill the fox (a necessary thing; a fortunate rationalization). A young one sets out in his own mirror-image, with *élan* and the environment-bossing steps of a conquistador and, this being 1961, and the context therefore unfruitful, slips on Ben's bridge and falls in the river. He went to Ben's farm to dry, and Ben laughed so much that he had to retire to his bedroom to finish his laughter in peace. Ben is the opposite of the conquistador. He lacks the jerky, eruptic and arhythmical emphasis of townspeople in his movements. They would appear clumsy to the narcissists of elegance; who are elegant out of context. Closer viewed they have a sinuous continuity subtly punctuated by the rhythm of perfect and functioning locomotion, like a line of good verse. His walk deals with the ground, not with an abstract principle of progress minted into the manners thereof. His walk does not attack the ground but, like the butcher Chuang-Tzu writes of, lovingly engages it to the advantage of his purpose. His speech is in the same kind, guarding its old-fashioned virtue, totally lacking in the spasms of constricted emotion. In this way countrymen, and notably Welshman, who are fluent, lusty and pretty fine physically, are superior in physical integration and harmony. Hence their song: the soul moves upon Welsh song as a dancer upon a ballroom floor. This is the *ease* of *dynamic* life: with release comes genius. It comfortably houses sometimes spectral derangement; it has no narrow anti-insanity, but a primordial synthesis. The East offers the same in its music. So, like the Jews, they see through all *avoirdupois* of 'majesty' bought from without: the Welshman is not built up by commodities; like the Jew, he becomes leaner, not fatter, in wealth, ever persisting in distinguishing his ego from his property—because the latter is strictly functional.

Ben and Dai Williams are to me pristine Welsh, guarded against all vulgarizing 'modernity' by an inscrutable taste of which they are quite unconscious because it cannot fail them. Their suspicion of strangers is without rancour: they watch, and do not communicate their deductions—probably not even to themselves. They live together in their farm, Croesor Bach, a little way up the mountain across the stream and opposite Bryn Hyfryd. Their house is the most home-like I have ever seen, grown around them like a suit of clothes, as has the building been grown around by the mountain. The *delicacy* of such a degree of integration would have delighted D. H. Lawrence; it was his favourite perception, and is best expressed in his descriptions of the ways of animals. This one thing is a flower of this world. Ben is mostly the guardian; Dai is the dreamer, more. Ben looks shrewd, the kind of man whom fools would consider simple in the pejorative sense; he is so in the positive sense—only. Dai looks very fresh, with eyes of startlingly clear blue—bits of sky—and once wrote a considerable amount of poetry, which he reads like Bach on the organ. His voice, like his brother's, is un-platformed: contrast it with the dizzy tiz of that of Hampstead cognoscenti. I heard a radio talk once about the unnatural and strained source of modern singing voices. Welsh, and the brothers' voices, confirm what the speaker said. Both brothers were born in their farm, and have never and will never move from it; their grandparents were there. Their dogs are wonderfully in keeping: Cwmru electric with nerve and loyalty, Black old-fashioned and deliriously loving. Cwmru's eyes are two flashes, and his tail like a national flag . . . of Wales.

The huntsman returns, blowing his horn. Why are huntsmen funny? Because they have the forms of might without the content, an anomaly like that of so many Shakespearian actors. Few things are as comic as a Briton on stage expressing power (always understood in the sense of destructive potential). The result is rhetoric of physical movement, like the rhetoric of the political speech. This pattern—dying in Edwardianism—appears in D. H. Lawrence's novels of the worst period—e.g. *The Plumed Serpent*. Also in his paintings; Lawrence painted husbands (stuffed power figures), never lovers. Power is no longer an attribute of the male body, but of the H-bomb and the machine; powerful men are pathetically old-fashioned in their *manners*. No doubt the viciousness of the toughs comes partly from a bewildering sub-consciousness of their anachronism. Little boys at school feel this. Poor power-man; he blows his little horn manfully up the mountain, and his respectful dogs, who have greater faith than we, answer this call. The English, and I suppose all 'great' peoples of a gone epoch, are the last to grow out of this power stereotype; in America it is frankly ludicrous, achieving neurotic status. Hence the sly humour of 'lesser' races, now in a position to take historical photographs of their one-time masters. The lesser races have been saved a short-term investment; they may approach mechanical power less competitively, less anthropomorphically, more maturely. The Welshman, like the Irishman, is in a good position here. In England the whole new embellishment (expressed in slogans of efficiency and 'drive', producing men with gimlet expressions) of the old ideology is most marked in the 'grammar-school' class—their superiors are a little slyer in adaptation. For them, power is still anachronistically an attribute of muscular prowess in the destructive sense: this makes for inefficiency, prevents the fruitful love of the machine (such as the Russians and, oddly enough, the Americans have). Britons still compete with their tools; partly because most Britons don't own them. Converse: Britons feel devilish when they drive cars. Neill, the teacher, brings up his children on other principles; rather, releases, brings to expression, the other principle of construction inherent in us. I met him recently; a truly great man.

January 16th

Nellie has a swollen finger and is pretty helpless, so Raymond, whom we call 'wicked', because he has the face of a Welsh angel out of which astute strategies are expressed, takes the day off from school. It is difficult to see what his help consists of; mostly moral, I suppose. This morning he was washing his bicycle by squirting water out of a bicycle pump over it, and he then washed the windows in the same way. He's a remarkable child, quick as the wind, doesn't like school very much because (I may have written this earlier) learning isn't yet grafted to intelligence, but makes a band around it. He has none of the dullness of penetration, all the quickness of observation, and doesn't yet live privately, but open to the elements and influences, which aren't quick enough to feed a brain out of his responses. He collapses sometimes with fury at the slowness of things. Len, his brother, is more conformist; calculates, has patience, and will do well. The steam engine is little Hefina—a scarlet bomb of a child in constant explosion. David, the eldest (who works on a farm), has an elegant soul and much wisdom; oddly evasive to the conventions; the environment is fairly propitious for that. He has a great tenderness. They're a chaotic family, often bawling the roof off; they totally lack interior hostility to each other, through a system of instant flash. Nellie manages them like a London policeman on traffic duty; she manages somehow to keep them in the right lanes, and if they get into the wrong ones she renames the lanes. She's a stupendously unworried-looking woman (being always conscious of minor worries), amazingly relaxed in the way that conventional women are tense. A glitter of critical humour is always in her eyes, showing how the back-brain can be more subtle than the front. She listens to anything, which is why it's easy to trip over oneself in talking to her: a conversation with her is like taking part in a piano and violin sonata. Of sexual goings-on she says: 'It's only natural,' an insight not general, though more common than elsewhere, among Croesorians. (Welsh humour is located in the crevasse between practice and precept). Nellie's respect for the Establishment is as sartorial as my trousers; it looks curiously naked. That which rich women seek from the analyst Nellie has; what great minds are after, what stunt-poets gnash false teeth in false grief at not having, she has. She has the best—inner peace. For she has not been privileged to prise two selves out of one and then learned to lament the breach. Spiritual adventure, the breaking up of the self in order to try and to fail in sticking it together again, is closed to her. So her effect is civilizing, quieting and soothing. Being a child, she is older in essentials than most adults. Her eyes are warm brown with the glitter-humour flickering always, her hair is black and grey, her face ruddy-tawny, and I trust she is a gypsy, but she may not be. Her body is small and quick and integrated in her character; the kind of body, blithe and without meanness, that has been a home to a man, not just a jousting partner. It has therefore dignity with comedy; true dignity is rarely without social comedy, reflecting the ineptness of social dignity. I hope she lives to a hundred unless she'd rather not. I hope also her radio, by losing a valve, will become quieter.

January 17th

Auntie Gwen arrived last night to see to Nellie's finger. Herewith a list of Auntie Gwen's activities:
1. Visits the bereaved.
2. Helps bring in children (to the world).
3. Village first-aid service (mobile—highly).
4. Runs hire-purchase club.

5. Cooks school meals.
6. Cleans for the Styleses.
7. Cleans chapel.
8. Plays organ therein.
9. Cleans school.
10. Supplies tomatoes and mushrooms.
11. Looks after children in summer.
12. Looks after resident old lady.

She's been seen cleaning the school at 3 a.m., reason being that her great flow of speech somewhat impedes her locomotion. She also collects for various charities. Health is good here, much longevity: a working farmer of over eighty, spry as a robin; a farmer of eighty-five publishes a poem about one of ninety-five just died. Nellie hasn't been ill for seventeen years, and her children won't be if they eat less sweets. Mrs. Morgan says we often miss the epidemics.

'We are all hypocrites,' says Bob Owen to me. He was referring to the discretion required when writing of people. Bob thinks *Lady C.* goes too far; the comic law case was under discussion. The four-letter word has been salvaged for hygiene, sex is nearly legal, hence the existence of the whole court nearly legal, and the creative exercises of their parents nearly legal, and themselves positively impinging upon life. A triumph for Puritanism so subtle that the prosecution didn't realize it was opting for continued obscenity by means of its essential suppression. So: sensual pleasure still inhabits the lower deck, driven all the more furiously there by its marionette facsimiles being allowed on the promenade. Not yet the head shall meet the heart or body; divine segregation! How will the permitted wraiths of lust now exercise in the legal light of day? Lust has now only one outlet: asceticism. But every decent man has known that all his adult life, ever since Puritans invented debauchery.

January 24th

Vision, maturity, enlightenment and intelligence in an ideal community: A bakes a cake for one of the frequent competitions here, but B's cake wins the prize: A does not speak to B for two or three years; all the time the river flows to the sea, and much happens in the world. The level of this is only to be found in one other field of human activity: international politics, with missiles instead of cakes.

Cwmru (Ben's dog) was picked up by the police at Llanfrothen, where he courts. He bit the policeman.

Welsh economy: one lady's electricity bill for the quarter (in summer) was 1s. 6d. Of course she rises and beds with the sun (*intacta*). It is said that the Welsh are 'mean'; I prefer to call them economical, which is the result of a very long experience of poverty that the Nationalist Party has no hesitation in, and some convincing arguments for, ascribing to English exploitation of the country. But this economy I find an extraordinarily attractive trait; it is not confined to money and property matters, but is also expressed in their wholly delightful concern with minutiae in life's matters generally. They are observant of tiny details; the miniature quality in the Northern Welsh landscape, which makes it so brilliantly clear and so crisply formed, is also to be seen at its source in the crinkled humour around the central vital spark of the Welsh eye, and the gnomelike quality of Welsh expression and rapid, close-formed gesture. It is a quality also to be found in the neat involution of Welsh design as well as in the intensely detailed discussion and commentary of our tradesmen; as though phenomena were butterflies awaiting the brilliance of Welsh pins. The quick and the small delight them, and their nimbleness and fluent response are mental characteristics as well of the people. We are forced to realize by contrast, here, the grossness endemic in all waste, and consequently beautiful appreciation of certain aspects of the world too liberally generalized in the considerations of more economically prosperous peoples. Welsh speech is also a clear river running over brilliantly individuated pebbles. From this we deduce the source of that sprung-rhythmical quality with which they are thoroughly informed, fully expressed in their song. The Welsh curve, like the Welsh curl in hair, eye, mouth, is wire-springy and glossily involuted; the only generalization is in the border, the context, protective against the incursive; within, trills know no inhibitions. There is thus a sense of the conspiratorial nature of life in which, to survive, one has respectfully to engage; one does not attack, but partakes organically in a conspiracy.

Welsh decoration lacks the large generalizing curves of English; that it is nearer the gaiety and prinking intimacy of some Italian architecture is made evident by the fittingness of Williams-Ellis's Italianate importations at Portmeirion. The tastebuds have not been educated all away, even if they have not yet been educated into their full expression; they curl like snails in the shell history has protectively lodged them in. We have a native culture still capable of prosperously reacting, freshly and characteristically, to the hazards of environment —however dormant it may seem, it is a case of cold storage and not of death. Its future may be curiously nascent, like those emergences into new worlds that are the core of D. H. Lawrence's perception; spring-time is not dead.

Nascence is the quality most noticeable in Bob Owen, who might, from one's impression of him, have been born any minute; who is perpetually born before one's eyes through the authentic freshness of his surprise and curiosity. Such a quality sings in the speech of John Thomas, the handsome, unhurrying hedger—a series of brief burps, or calls, in riverine rhythms, his light eyes, beautifully arched, flickering with amusement at the happy act of speech. Most of all you hear it in the children's voices, running like hedge-tops by a car, an absolute bowl of birdcalls, bright as flint on flint, with a cheery, chuckling sound; the children are universally amused. So sterling is the Welsh core that they can afford, in that security suggestive of a young people, to be amused at living; even the veils of Methodism are ruffled in this breeze, being lightly worn by most.

Being no nation of shopkeepers, honour more than honesty attracts them; the difference is fine, their choice the sweeter. For honour is the best carving on the human face of the temporal rock; honesty niggles in internalized courts. I do not mean that they are dishonest; I mean they *do* confuse the cross of Calvary with a grocer's bill. Honour gleams purest; for honesty is degenerated to a strategy in the game whose goal, we fear, is otherwise.

Their honour is (to us) quaint—rather 'trodle-ish' [*sic*], and enjoyed by repetition, always the mode of basic education. For instance, at the Penrhyn pub I am told that quite regularly Ben will ask for 'six hundredweight of potatoes', by which he means six packets of potato crisps; such is Ben's social criticism, flower of his sense of economy.

Epilogue

HAD I written this book later, after having been here longer and having known the place and the people better, it would certainly have been different. It would have been either a sociological study or a conventionally 'insightful' account of people in a small odd place. As it is, it at times strikes me as being lyrical, romantic, idealizing. But I do not partake of the current myth that the grey is the realistic, that realism is an exercise in what you don't like; and I do not think that the less 'pleasant' aspects of people are more important than the 'pleasant' aspects. I think, in fact, that the good things are more realistic, whereas the bad are more historical. What could it profit me, or you, to know what we know—that gossip, malice, acquisitiveness, are to be found here as everywhere in the world? That isn't news; what is more news is that certain lyrically expressive characteristics of individuals exist below these cliché attributes of us all; that, in a word, man wears his 'evil' to protect, contain, deploy his 'good'. But we have of course to refine 'good' away from much of the conventionally moral associated with it, which is as fashionable as the 'bad'. 'Good' I would define as the essentially pacific desire to live; 'bad' is where, in a poor systematic arrangement, it meets similar desires and has to compete with them. Bad is an economic, systematic fatality; good conquers.

We say with too much rhetoric that man is good; the cult of human advertising, in its ineptness, shows a good deal of suspicion of the proposition. Is 'man' 'good'? 'It depends upon what you mean.' He is not good in that he accepts the need to travel along social rails whose passage and destination are temporary and socially exigent at the moment; out of that not-goodness comes his wickedness. But he is good in that (1) he is the inventor of the concept and (2) that he is . . . alive. Life is greater, thank heaven, than morality, which so often seems specifically invented to put it out, and nearly always to shade it. Every epoch has its virtue, its moral code; in the present, not stealing, working, not fighting, seem to be the thing. But those qualities are not yet grand enough to approximage to the nature of men. Stealing is a technicality; work is an exigency; not fighting—well, only a belligerent world could invent such a virtue (a highly necessary one). No. The nature of man is other: I'd hint at it as being expansive up to some apogee, then absorbent to dissolution. Man's development is a process of increasing consciousness, which means the anticipation of all events through knowledge, which means the search for creative dissolution into his ever-present origins. That which promotes this is, therefore, good: but the dialectical process makes the moral valuation of any one phase too difficult—all contribute, obviously, and the sum always lies ahead. And societies cannot be better than nurseries of intuition towards the end.

We may call the present epoch 'bad' because it elevates the accidental into the dramatic, the anarchic into the free, the planless into the libertarian; whereas planlessness is bondage, anarchy is—alas—false in all its forms because all its forms are premature anticipations of heaven to come on earth; and the accidental is the uncouth from which even poets are hard driven to cull a lyric. It is a bad epoch because it presumes to a civilization hard, at times, to believe to be even within its reach. It is bad because it inflates individuals into anti-social personalities, those dripping public fountains of unenlightenment enough to turn one away from the human race. It is bad because it does not see that the common is greater than the uncommon, that the greatly hopeful human qualities are qualities possessed of all people, upon which the *legitimately* extraordinary may be built; because it does not see that true individualism is the flower of community, and that the kind we have is but an atrophied simulacrum of what we shall one day have; because competition is waste at *every* level.

But pessimism is wrong because, though it sees our poor state, it deduces (or contrives) therefrom a human principle; whereas we have merely a historical series of events. This is what has happened, it is not as we are. So, the realist (miscalled the optimist) will refuse to see waste even in the organization of waste called society. He will instead speculate and proclaim upon the contributions of error to truth: for they work hand in hand.

Could men *bother*, as a species, to be bad? They are not civilized for so enormous a degree of organization and conditioning required! Neither can we truly say they are good and bad, or neither. They are good: but good is not yet defined for the new age, though its anticipatory blue-print—Christianity—is with us, and its technical plan—socialism—is also with us. But the ethics of the future are as yet only dreamed of; ethics for a world of non-competitive human beings reaching out to the universe.

Which is the point of this village, Croesor. 'Accidentally', Croesor is competitively backward. Therefore it well accommodates the dream of things to come. To return to my starting point, the immediate, 'optimistic', rosy view of the people is more realistic, more correct, than the dingier, greyer, more 'profound' view that would have come later. Catch it, it may have been put to me, in the bud of your perception of it. That is what I have tried to do.